BEYOND
IDEOLOGY

BEYOND IDEOLOGY

A Christian Response to Sociopolitical Conflict in Asia

WON SUL LEE

Cornerstone Books
Westchester
Illinois 60153

BEYOND IDEOLOGY: A Christian Response
to Sociopolitical Conflict in Asia

Copyright ©1979 by Cornerstone Books,
a division of Good News Publishers
Westchester, Illinois 60153
All rights reserved.
Printed in the United States of America.

Library of Congress Catalog Card Number 78-71944
ISBN 0-89107-163-6

Contents

Foreword

Dr. Won Sul Lee, a Third World leader, trained on both sides of the Pacific, brings to this volume a combination of scholarship and spirituality unique.

No Westerner, no matter how thoroughly trained in cultural anthropology, international relations, behavioral sciences, history and related fields, could possibly match the accuracy of perceptions contained in *Beyond Ideology*. The Korean language edition has already been enthusiastically received in colleges, universities and seminaries in Korea. Incidentally, there are more Th.D.'s per capita in Korea than any nation in the world, including the United States.

I rejoice that Dr. Lee has felt the divine mandate to carve out the time and invest the energy required to produce this most important treatise. No one—the most casual layman included—interested in the Third World will be able to put this book down once he has started reading the initial pages.

John Haggai, Director
The Haggai Institute

Preface

Asia means different things to different people. For geographers, it is a term delineating the vast land mass stretching from the Middle East to Northeast Russia. For historians, it is the cradle of many ancient civilizations. For economists, it is an area comprising many underdeveloped and developing countries. For political scientists, it consists of newly emergent nations struggling to modernize their societies. For most Westerners, Asia means a way of life antithetical to that of the West.

Of late, Asia has attracted the attention of thinking people in all fields for a host of new reasons. Today's Asia is utterly chaotic and almost without hope. Reports from this part of the world continuously bring news of wars, riots, *coups*, and famine. All sorts of tensions, both hidden and apparent, are seething just below the surface, ready to break out into lethal conflicts at any moment, at any place, and on any issue. In contrast, we find that at the same time Asia is on the move, boldly and steadfastly making progress in every realm of human life. Never before have Asians been as confident, enterprising, and forward-looking as they are today. Of these two opposing scenes which is the true picture of Asia?

For Christians, however, Asia has a more significant meaning. Of the forty billion people living on earth, about 56.7 percent are in Asia, as compared to 6 percent in North America, 8.1 percent in Latin America, 12.1 percent in

Europe, 6.5 percent in Russia, 10.1 percent in Africa, and 0.5 percent in Oceania. Six of the world's ten major cities are in Asia. Without evangelizing Asia, there is no way for us to fulfill the Great Commission of our Lord. Yet the current situation of Asia makes Christians feel intimidated. Today, this vast area is a battleground of sociopolitical ideologies, the ground where the future destiny of mankind may well be determined. Furthermore, the resurgence of old traditional religions is everywhere apparent.

Can the rate of evangelization in Asia keep abreast of the explosive growth of population? Can Christianity, which has often been branded as a part of Western imperialism, cope with the challenge of "secular gospels" such as Communism? Will the Christian church be able to withstand the formidable counterattack of traditional Asian religions such as Hinduism, Buddhism, Confucianism, and Shintoism? Can Christians prevail against the rising tide of secularism? Can we demonstrate that the Gospel is not only for individual salvation but also for genuine, lasting social and cultural progress?

To provide serious answers to these serious questions is a herculean task, one which certainly is beyond the scope of this work. In dealing with the present complex Asian situation, a writer, no matter how perceptive, cannot be free from making misjudgments. In the midst of pandemonium a man's intellectual vista is too limited and his historical perspective too narrow. Nevertheless, as an Asian Christian historian reared in the dust of tumultuous transformation, I now feel compelled to express some Christian views on these problems. In this work I have made an attempt to relate my Christian beliefs to the actual condition of life surrounding me in Asia.

The gist of my ideas is that the historical progress that we Asians are so eager to make cannot be realized by the application of futuristic sociopolitical ideologies (futurism) or by the revival of anachronistic traditional religions (archaism). Nor will it be achieved by the autonomic laws of dialectical process. On the contrary, genuine cultural growth is a byproduct of our spiritual life which seeks to follow the will of God. Matthew 6:33 says, "But seek ye first the kingdom of God, and his righteousness, and all these things shall be added unto you." To me, this is the only way for transfiguring the Asian milieu.

I must make it clear at the outset that my writing tends to be inevitably normative. In diagnosing the current situation of Asia, I often make sweeping generalizations before expressing my opinions, if not suggested remedies, and they are largely drawn from the world of ought-to-be, namely the teaching of the Bible. Always, there is inherent danger in making generalizations, the danger of either too-much or too-little, and there are even more hazards in discussing answers in normative terms. Yet, here too, there can be a justification. A writer who minimizes generalization and withholds his opinions perhaps should be castigated. After all, what is he writing for?

Every thinking man, every mortal endowed with limited vision, is bound to make mistakes. But the mistakes he makes can often be a foundation on which others may build their new intellectual edifices. Paradoxically enough, in this very capacity to make misjudgments lies man's ability to fulfill himself and to develop society. I feel that if some Christian intellectuals, even a few, find interesting or polemic points to discuss as a result of reading this work, my efforts will be amply rewarded.

1

Asian Upheaval

Asia, the erstwhile land of serenity, is now caught in a revolutionary fever unprecedented in history. All the varied revolutions which gradually transformed the West over the centuries following the Renaissance are at work simultaneously in this part of the world. The winds of change have become so strong that nothing seems to remain immutable. Commercial revolution, agricultural revolution, industrial revolution, intellectual revolution, scientific-technological revolution, social revolution, feminist revolution, and even generational revolution are in the making throughout this vast and turbulent continent, producing abundant blessings and immeasurable curses, all at the same time. What we are experiencing in today's Asia is a total revolution, different from previous historical changes not only in degree, but also in kind.

Ironically enough, though, when we look beyond the surface phenomena, we find that the ancient traditions—both the desirable and the abhorrent—remain strong. Viewed in the light of history, no country of Asia has really changed. Beneath the hustle and bustle of modernization, the old Asia remains unmolested. It is true that the introduction of new political institutions, social systems, industrial operations, and technological innovations has drastically modified the physical appearance of the area. But the elements of modernization float on the surface and have not penetrated the deep psychic substrata of the Asian mind.

1. DYNAMICS OF CHANGE AND CONTINUITY

Contradictions abound within every Asian society. The antithetical signs of progress and retrogression, vitality and decay, and hope and despair are inextricably intertwined in confusion. The myriad of contradictory phenomena, pervasive throughout Asia in spite of the heterogeneous cultural heritages and sociopolitical differences among the respective societies, stem from an overall antinomic fact. Two paradoxical postulates appear to be equally founded in reality: 1) Asia is in a constant flux of changes and nothing here remains unchanged, and 2) despite the seemingly revolutionary concussion, Asia has not really changed and everything remains basically the same.

The political realm provides a striking example. Self-contradictory phenomena have become increasingly evident in Asian politics. Due to the lofty goals of achieving individual and collective political freedom, most Asian nations in the postwar era have carried out political revolutions, making this continent the center of contemporary revolutions. The first wave of political revolutions, the national revolutions for independence in the 1940s, was followed by a second wave in the 1960s. The governments which had been led by such outstanding founding fathers as Syngman Rhee, U Nu, Ngo Dinh Diem, and Sukarno were thrown out. During the 1960s, even Mao Tse-tung had to purge his political enemies in the name of the "Cultural Revolution" in order to remain in power; and the government of the Liberal-Democratic Party in Japan, seemingly the most stable in Asia, was seriously challenged by the *Zenkaguren* and other left-wingers. The resurgence of the Pathet Lao, the Free Thai, and the Huks in the same decade also revealed the political instability of Asian nations. Now, standing in the second half of the 1970s, we see crises erupting again in many Asian countries, as is so well demonstrated by the critical condition of Thailand. There are convincing reasons to expect more political turmoil in Asia in the foreseeable future.

Meanwhile, in order to safeguard individual rights and human freedom, many democratic institutions—such as the parliament, judiciary systems, political parties, and electoral mechanisms patterned after the West—have been introduced, remodeled, and often refurbished according to the demand of changing times. Innumerable elections have been held, usually with a high percentage of voters taking part in them. Such technical terms as inalienable rights, bill of rights, *habeas corpus*, referendum, and recall have now become household words among Asians. What then is the degree of political maturity of Asian nations today?

To a certain degree, there has been political development in every Asian society. Even the uneducated masses have begun to claim their inherent rights as human beings, and the governments have become much more efficiently institutionalized in processing the political demands of people. But in reality, are we Asians freer than we were before? Contrary to what had been expected, "Oriental despotism" has not declined; it has merely assumed some sophisticated modern forms. The specter of Leviathan—the authoritarian, dictatorial, despotic, and totalitarian states employing elaborate equipment and methods for mass intimidation and mass manipulation—gulps the freedom of people, both politically and psychologically. The masses are swiftly *apoliticized* by the ruling elite. Popular sovereignty in many Asian countries has become a sham.

Equally contradictory dynamics of change and continuity can be found in the economic realm of Asian life. On one hand, most Asian societies have raised their standard of living. No longer is Asia the land of timeless peasants tilling the muddy soil in a vicious circle of poverty and hunger. In their desire to hurry and catch up with the West, every Asian nation has carried out a series of long- and short-term economic development plans for industrialization. Granted that some of the statistical figures published by governments are exaggerated, the rate of economic growth, even taking into account the relatively small size of the national economy in most Asian nations, has surpassed that of the advanced societies of the West. According to figures made available by the United Nations, the industrial output of Asia expanded almost tenfold during the past two decades[1]. South Korea, for instance, has maintained an average of 11 percent GNP growth annually over the past fifteen years.

With extremely limited national capital and meager technological skill, and amid the rapidly fluctuating international power configuration ranging from bipolarization to multi-polarization, what Asian nations have achieved during the postwar era is impressive. And though new mega-cities thrive, attracting more and more people to urban life, the chronic problems accompanying rapid urbanization plague Asia. Furthermore, industrial pollutants vex Asian countries as much as they trouble the West.

One common ideology underlying all the economic development plans has been egalitarianism, the idea which ignited the "revolution of expectation" among the masses. For the sake of an affluent tomorrow, people were asked to sacrifice today. Adamant and undaunted in the face of seemingly insurmountable difficulties and obstacles, they have done exactly that. As a result, the level of economic well-being has risen considerably.

Is economic egalitarianism then becoming a reality? No amount of "economic showcases"—rising industrial plants, highways, hydroelectric dams, and skyscrapers—can, however, hide the growing frustration of the Asian masses who are more often than not passed over in the distribution of wealth. The rich get richer while the poor remain indigent. Both in Communist and non-Communist countries, the toiling masses are equally and viciously exploited, working for wages far below the basic subsistence level.

Worse still, the middle class has no strong native roots. In many cases, the so-called capitalists in Asia were, and to some extent, still are compradors, people working for foreign firms. Beset by the lack of capital and technological skills and strangled by the inroads of neocolonial expansion by multinational corporations from the big powers, Asians still have a long way to go before attaining self-reliance. The growing viability of the national bourgeoisie in each society is undeniable. But relying too heavily on the subsidies and privileges granted by government, the bulk of Asian businessmen still belong to the category of "government-manufactured entrepreneurs," who live parasitically on bureaucracy.

Furthermore, business organizations and business practices have not been modernized. Behind the facade of modern business structures which generally take the form of the Western corporation lies the old mentality of familism in the form of "informal organizations." These aim at the tight control of firms on the traditional pattern. Little business ethics has grounded its roots in Asia. Consequently, because it has no spiritual foundation, the present economic modernization of Asia may well be compared to building on a foundation of sand.

Socially, the elements of change and continuity have become more pronounced. In the postwar era every Asian society has experienced at least a twofold mobility, spatial and vertical. On one hand, Asian societies have become increasingly mobile as a result of an unprecedented rate of social changes caused by industrialization and urbanization. Also, a series of wars—including the Korean War, the Vietnamese War, the Laotian War, and the Khmer War—has produced vast movements of people in a modern form of exodus, leaving deep-rooted sociopsychological effects. On the other hand, an equally striking vertical mobility—changes in social stratification—is taking place. As the spatial movement of people resulted in social mobility, class cleavages could not remain sacrosanct: petty merchants are becoming rich industrialists in the same manner in which peasant boys, by virtue of military careers, rapidly climbed the social ladder.

As the Asian societies suddenly became fluid, the old, decadent ruling classes of each society, enervated and spiritless, could not remain unchallenged. The old rajahs, aristocrats, sultans, mandarins, and seigneurs gave way to the rise of a new breed of leaders. A large number of today's Asian leaders have lower-class origins, and therefore show that the present chaotic social conditions provide men of talent and ambition with ample opportunity for upward social mobility.

The pattern of upward social mobility has not, however, been stabilized yet, and over the years it has created many serious problems. For instance, as spatial and vertical social mobility accelerates, sectional-communal-clannish feelings, instead of diminishing as originally expected, become intensified, for—because of the increasing physical contact caused by the shrinkage of the time-spatial dimension of life—the psychological gaps separating different groups have become widened. After leaving their primary groups in the rural sector, people who moved into large cities became swiftly atomized, with practically no regrouping into secondary groups based upon mutual interests. All in all, the traditional social structure has become seriously deranged and dangerously decomposed, but no new structure has emerged to replace the old.

Hidden under the surface phenomena and deeper in its far-reaching consequence is the dynamics of change and continuity in the Asian psyche. The traditional Asians, regardless of minor differences among various groups, are perhaps best exemplified by Lao-tzu, the founder of Taoism. His goal in life was nonaction, the achieving of harmony with nature. All the social, political, economic, and cultural institutions have revolved around this ideal of harmony with nature. The *Weltanschauung* of Hinduism and Buddhism was basically pessimistic and unworldly. Confucianism had a more positive outlook on life, but it advocated the status quo, certainly not rapid social change.

In contrast, after passing through the turmoil of revolutionary historical changes over the decades, the typical Asian of today is quite the opposite of the traditional type—so different that he has become restless, impatient, acquisitive, this-worldly, and aggressive, seeking change at the expense of status quo. The modern Asian is likened to Faust. No longer is Confucianism a sacred cow in the minds of young Chinese, Koreans, or Japanese. Buddhism is not so revered among the youth of the Buddhist countries in Southeast Asia. Nor does Hinduism remain sacrosanct as it once was in the minds of Indian youths. An anti-Confucianism movement has vigorously been at work in Mao's China.

The value revolution, especially among the youth, goes on, subtly but vigorously, intensifying among other things the generational conflict between the old and the young. Historically, the problem of generational cleavage arising from value changes is not new. It is alluded to even in the ancient Babylonian myth of Tiamat and Marduk. But with the speed of historical change so accelerated the way it is today, the generations within the time dimension have become so drastically different in thinking and behavior that practically no intelligent communication between the old and the young is possible. While the old still honor traditional values and ideals, reckless Asian youth are ready to change everything to modernize their society. In their efforts to emulate Western values, however, they often lose their self-identity, finding they belong neither to the East nor to the West. If they defy their traditional values as servile moral doctrines, can they give blanket approval of Western values? The answer is no.

In their feeling of an identity separate from the older generation and in their opposition to traditionalism, Asian youth appears to be not very different from Western youth. Both speak slang, sing sensual songs, enjoy rock 'n' roll, grow long hair, and often act violently. But their similarities

are more apparent than real. Western youth living in affluence are not overwhelmingly concerned with physical survival, material security, and social status. Their opposition
against the well-lubricated machine-like society in which
they exist almost meaninglessly is "metamotivational." In
sharp contrast, the generational revolution of Asia can be
called "motivational." Having had no experience of living
in affluence, young people in Asia, except perhaps in Japan,
have a great desire to possess something tangible; and having no hope of getting what they want, they blame the
leaders in their societies, especially those in politics, and
undertake radical actions. In brief, youth in Asia oppose
traditionalism and establishments, but at the same time are
loath to accept Western values. Thus, they find no alternative values of their own.

More evidence of the value dilemma can be seen in the
feminist revolution which, too, is smoldering, making ir-
reversible breakthroughs against male chauvinism. Woman
is no longer regarded as man's appendage. The status of
Asian women in the past was well described in a classical
Chinese poem which said, "How sad it is to be women,
nothing on earth is held so cheap." But the situation has
now changed considerably, if not completely, as can be
seen in Malaysia, a Moslem country, where even the king
could not take an additional wife because of the strong protest of women. Although sexual equality is still a goal, not a
reality, many Asian women on their own individual merits
have ascended the social ladder, presently holding important positions as teachers, doctors, technicians, scientists,
artists, and even premiers. Due to increasing educational
opportunities and the availability of more jobs because of
industrialization, more prominent women leaders will appear in all fields of society in the future.

However, along with these hopeful changes arise many
unexpected and undesirable problems—problems such as a
rising divorce rate, sexual promiscuity, the increase in the
number of unwed mothers and abandoned children, and

the decline in family ties. Young girls, after escaping from their rural communities and migrating aimlessly to the large cities, often fall into the traps of the sexual and economic slave market. Women's liberation has ironically produced more problems than solutions.

If viewed in terms of continuity, therefore, changes in the value hierarchy in today's Asia must be regarded as superficial and, in the long run, ephemeral. Traditional values are very strong even in such industrially advanced societies as Japan, where, for instance, Yukio Mishima, an internationally renowned writer, committed hara-kiri in samurai tradition to arouse Japanese militarism. Even in the suicidal attacks of the so-called Japanese Red Army in Israel and in Europe do I find the resuscitating Japanese samurai spirit. This is to say that in spite of the intellectual modernization which has been going on in Asia for decades, little in fact has changed in the realm of spirit. The majority of Asian peoples still adhere to traditional values. Even today, Morarji Desai, who once served as finance minister of India, says that he believes "in astrology as a science," for "one's destiny is the sum-total of the consequence of one's past life."[2]

Asis is experiencing a multidirectional revolution which ironically sets no real goal for forward movement. How has Asia been thrown into this chaos? Let us now delve into history to find the reasons for this.

2. OSCILLATION OF TRADITIONALISM AND WESTERNISM

The question as to what factors and forces are causing the revolutionary dynamics of change and continuity in today's Asia, creating such diversified and contradictory phenomena, cannot be answered with mathematical formulas. Historical causes and effects are so inextricably entangled as to make a simplistic generalization impossi-

ble. However, in spite of the danger in making generalizations, we may surmise that the historical metamor-
phosis of today's Asia began, in fact, originally at the time
when Asian civilizations were challenged by the West.

Needless to say, the geographical area known as Asia
contains many different ethnic groups, religions, nations,
and civilizations. Or in larger categories, Asia is made up of
a few great cultural units such as the Indic culture, the Sinic
culture, and the Moslem culture, with diversified and often
dramatically divergent *Weltanshauungs*. Inasmuch as the
term Asia was of Greek origin, appearing first in Pindar's
poems in the sixth century B.C., and was introduced to
China perhaps by Matteo Ricci only in the sixteenth century
A.D., there was no collective psyche known as the "Asian
consciousness" as such. Every civilization had a different
set of beliefs and values which we call today ethos. Through
the millennia, these great traditions, supported and upheld
by the equally great systems of thought such as Hinduism,
Buddhism, Confucianism, and Taoism, changed extremely
slowly.

As Eugene Kamenka points out, "Revolution has come to
Asia because Europe has come to Asia."[3] The Hobson-
Lenin thesis of imperialism, despite its profound insights,
cannot depict the whole multifarious, complicated picture
of Western expansion, which in effect was "one of the far-
reaching consequences of that magnificent outburst of the
energy which turned against the decaying stagnant
societies of the non-European world."[4] In retrospect, the
West could launch such a formidable, tidal challenge upon
the East because it had become modern. Admittedly, the
term *modern* is not well defined, for it is not a set of fixed
social systems, but the dynamic process of change—"a persistent capacity for coping with a permanent change."[5]
Under the influence of the West, the traditional political
systems, social norms and mores, ethical values, and
thought of Asian civilizations were seriously challenged
and dangerously deranged. Many new roads, railways,

small-scale factories, and schools were constructed under Western domination, and new concepts of law and government were introduced. Asia was drawn into the modernizing revolution.

In no way do I, however, mean to imply that Asian societies were modernized by Western challenge alone. Formidable as it was, the Western challenge did not, and probably could not, transform the traditional societies of Asia into modernity. The economic exploitation, political suppression, and intellectual intimidation the Western powers used in Asia were inexcusable, unjustifiable, and unpardonable. Furthermore, as Robert Sinai observes, the Western impact on Asian societies remained "fundamentally a superficial one, affecting only the shallow upper layer of the Asian traditional ways of life."[6] What really began to shake Asia from the bottom was not so much the exogenous forces generated by Western challenge as the internal forces arising in Asian psyches. It is therefore important for us to see the modes of Asian response to the Western challenge, if possible, in a chronological sequence of historical events.

To trace the historical course of the Asian response to the West of individual nations is beyond the scope of this work, for according to different ethics, each nation reacted differently. At this juncture, speculative and metahistorical as it is, we may deal with the course of Asian reawakening in terms of a pattern of dialectical growth, which in our case appears in the rhythmic cycle of the yin (negative) and yang (positive).

This is to say that in spite of the individual uniqueness of human events, we find in history some discernible regularities, some rhythms, some uniformities, some patterns in the course of the Asian awakening which may arbitrarily be called the cycle of Westernism and Traditionalism. After the advent of the West, the traditional leaders of Asia invariably turned against the invasion of Western ideas, customs, and institutions for some time. But in due course men of foresight began to accept such Western ideologies as democracy and nationalism, together with scientific thoughts, in their efforts, ironically, to fight against the West. And then, later, another nativistic reaction set in against Western learning in the form of a renaissance of Eastern learning. Viewed broadly on a macrocosmic scale, Asian history in the modern era can be delineated in a chronological pattern with four periods of the Traditionalism-and-Westernism cycle as shown in the following:

1. *The first cycle*—from the 16th century to the mid-19th century;
2. *The second cycle*—from the late 19th century to 1945;
3. *The third cycle*—from 1945 to 1960;
4. *The fourth cycle*—from 1960 to the present.

Long before the arrival of Vasco da Gama in India in 1498, Marco Polo and some Franciscan friars came to China for trading and evangelization. But it was not until the early sixteenth century when the rising new monarchs of the West sought new territorial expansion that the Western challenge became a serious threat to Asian countries. Politically fragmented and militarily powerless, India failed to show any creative response to the Western challenge and, by the eighteenth century, had become a hapless bone of contention between Great Britain and France. Likewise, the old kingdoms of Java and Sumatra fell to Western colonialism, first to Portugal and later to the Netherlands. Likewise the Philippines, which was hopelessly divided among rivaling tribes, had no centripetal force to resist the Spanish conquistadors.

The First Cycle
In contrast, China, Japan, Burma, Thailand, and Vietnam showed much more viability in resisting the Western challenge, eventually unfolding the pattern of the yin-yang rhythmic cycle in their responses. At first, the traditional rulers of these countries, with thoughts of their own cul-

tural superiority still lingering in their minds, looked down upon the West, believing that their ways of life, particularly in the spiritual realm, were basically superior to Western civilization. Although the West in the sixteenth century was going through the great modernizing transformation known in history as the Renaissance-Reformation, the emergent modern Western states, still in a preindustrial stage of historical development, had no preponderant power, economic or military, over these Asian countries.

On this equal, or slightly superior, footing, the Ming court of China, for instance, readily welcomed the opportunities to learn about Western technology in the sixteenth century—technology as exemplified by the clock, the map, the calendar, and the cannon. Matteo Ricci and other Catholic missionaries gained some limited success in preaching the Gospel. But by the seventeenth century, largely because of the "rites controversy" between the Dominicans and the Franciscans over their different attitude toward ancestral worship in Chinese tradition, a strong nativistic reaction against Christianity set in, resulting in the expulsion of Westerners from the Celestial Empire of the Ch'ing Dynasty.

A similar phenomenon of the yin-yang cycle became evident in Japan. In the mid-sixteenth century when Francis Xavier and other Catholic missionaries arrived, some warring feudal daimio readily accepted Christianity and guns from the West, and by 1600 there were more than 300,000 Christians in Japan. By the seventeenth century, however, with the Tokugawa family's hegemony firmly established, Japanese Christians were ruthlessly exterminated. In the meantime, in Southeast Asia, the Westernism-and-Traditionalism cycle followed more irregular, but basically similar, patterns. Both in Vietnam and in Burma, Western influence, mainly through French Catholic missionaries, was strongly felt until the eighteenth century, but for various political reasons, reaction against the West set in rapidly in the following century.

The Second Cycle

The second period of the yin-yang cycle, according to my arbitrary chart, began in the 1860s and lasted until the end of World War II in 1945. This period was a direct result of the second wave of Western challenge which actually took place in the mid-nineteenth century, with the industrialized West possessing preponderant power over the still-agrarian Asian countries. Compared to the early Western colonial expansion in terms of the three C's (commerce, colony, and Christianity), the new imperialistic expansion of the nineteenth century in the form of the three G's (gold, glory, and God) was far more formidable and proved to be lethal. When China, the sleeping tiger, tried to resist Great Britain in the Opium War, she was, even to her own surprise, relentlessly humiliated. The Sepoy Rebellion of the Indians against British rule was mercilessly crushed. Suddenly, the old, formerly powerful Asian nations were awakened to the brutal reality of the world. Either they had to learn from the West to ward off Western influence, or they would perish.

The most phenomenal example of Westernization during this period was seen in the post-Meiji Restoration era of Japan. An insular nation with a long tradition of cultural borrowing, Japan, at the arrival of Commodore Matthew Perry in the Edo Bay in 1853 with his tiny naval squadron, readily reacted to the challenge by destroying the decadent feudal system dominated by the Tokugawa Shogunate. Thus, after 1868 the new breed of Japanese leaders, mostly young and ambitious, carried out a twofold transformation of their nation within an amazingly short span of time—industrialization on the Western model and sanctification of some traditional spiritual heritages such as emperor worship. China, too, after suffering repeated defeats, had to abandon her blind reactionalism against the West. In the post-Arrow War period, beginning around the 1860s, she again became receptive to Western learning. Although, because of her bulky size and long tradition, China could not transform herself as speedily as Japan, the Hundred Days Reform of Kang Yu-wei and the Empress Dowager's Reform at the turn of the century brought about some major changes in military, education, laws, and administration. Finally in 1911 the inept Ch'ing Dynasty was overthrown by the Double Ten Revolution.

Korea took a slightly varied course. In spite of the decadent Yi Dynasty, the ruling *yangban* class, which played triple roles as landlords, scholars, and bureaucrats, was quite resistant to the repeated challenge of Western powers. But by 1882, with the conclusion of the Korean-American Amity and Commercial Treaty, some progressive *yangban* youth like Kim Ok Kyun, after observing the Japanese Meiji Restoration, took revolutionary action against the *ancien regime*. The Tonghak, despite their nationalistic prejudices against Western learning, also demanded drastic changes in all realms of Korean life. By the turn of the century, the Independent Club—a political vehicle of the new breed of Korean intellectuals—pressed for more elaborate programs of reform. Even after the Japanese annexation of 1910, the upsurge of yang forces did not die out, and in their struggle against Japanese imperialism, many Korean leaders continued to draw ideas and ideals for their nationalism from Western tradition.

In South and Southeast Asia, we see the Westernism-and-Traditionalism cycle in a more subtle and gradual form. Here, by the late nineteenth century, all the countries except Thailand were under Western colonial rule, but the very nature of colonial systems, however well they might have been contrived, was bound to create opposition. In order to exploit the natives economically, the colonial powers had to introduce something new to their colonies. Transportation and communication had to be improved, new administrative systems had to be developed, and, most important, modern education had to be introduced to train the natives for various skills. Modernization in some realms of life was forced upon the people.

The newly rising intellectuals of this region began to take on modern roles as civil servants, doctors, engineers, skilled workers, lawyers, teachers, poets, and religious leaders. As a consequence, regardless of their professional differences, they began to share a new mentality very different from that of their forefathers, and, with new intellectual insight, to realize that the Westerners, despite their democratic and liberal traditions, were not treating them as equals. In civil service, the natives could not get promotions beyond a certain level; in business, they could not take part in decision-making; and in medical practice, they could not compete against Western doctors. In this deep frustration lay the source of their national consciousness.

These reawakening souls constituted a tiny fragment of each society, and the masses, still very ignorant, could not perceive what went on. Small in number and powerless though they were, they had cultural mobility and eventually became agents of change. As time went by, the individual efforts of these awakened souls were channeled into organizations ranging over a wide spectrum of interests, from religious and cultural to the outright political groups. In spite of their heterogeneous origins, they were all united in their nationalism, Asia's new sacred cow, which was modeled on Western concepts of nationalism.

The yang phase of this period persisted, steadfastly sparking many political-cultural movements such as the March First Movement of Korea and the May Fourth Movement of China, both in 1919, and many other similar nationalistic uprisings in Southeast and South Asia during the same period. The second major Asian political ideology, Communism, was introduced by the early 1920s. Up until that time, despite the presence of some intellectual Marxists, Communism as an organized power did not emerge in Asia, partly because of the obvious fact that the Asian societies, being so agrarian, had little of the proletariat revolutionary basis that Karl Marx described. But after the consolidation of the Bolshevik Revolution in Russia, the situation changed somewhat. For one thing, Lenin, in his famous strategy of the "flank attack," stirred up the Asians against Western imperialism and Japanese imperialism by the Karakhan Manifestoes of 1919 and 1920, and he dispatched Comintern agents such as Gregory Voitinsky to Asia. The Chinese Communist Party was inaugurated in Shanghai in 1921, and similar movements sprouted in many other Asian countries.

In comparison with nationalism, Communism enjoyed no mass following. Such doctrines as the class struggle were alien to the Asian soul and repugnant to nationalists. These weaknesses were substantially counterbalanced, however, by the watertight organization, the skillful strategy, the adroit adaptability, and the well-defined programs of Communist parties, which were in large measures tightly controlled, in a clandestine manner, by the Kremlin. In due course Communism presented itself to the Asians as a new secular gospel—a gospel which, with its all-encompassing philosophy of human existence, claimed to be a panacea for all ills.

But the yin phase of this second period, according to my chronological chart, began about the late 1920s when, because of the global depression, world powers became unduly chauvinistic.

In Japan, the threat of nationalistic reaction against Western liberalism became increasingly evident as the "party governments" failed to cope with the rising economic crises created by the worldwide depression. Fanatic chauvinists took over the reins of government in the 1930s with a series of political assassinations and eradicated the residue of Western liberalism in Japan. In China, the Nationalist Government, with its emphasis on paternalism, obedience, and state power, drew more and more of its spiritual sources from Confucianism. In Indonesia, the resurgence of traditionalism was strongly expressed by the Sarekat Islam movement, which stressed values different from Western values and beliefs. On the political plane, the birth of the

Indonesian Nationalist Party led by Sukarno in 1929 marked another milestone in the people's resistance to everything that Dutch colonial rule had introduced.

In Burma the Saya San rebellion against British rule in 1930-31 presaged a strong nationalist upsurge, and the Thakin Party, with its traditional ideals and values, became a new rallying point for intellectuals like Aung San and U Nu. The same was the case in Thailand. Largely because of the rapidly changing international power configuration caused by the rise of Fascism, Nazism, and Japanese militarism, coupled with the nation's deteriorating economic condition, a military revolution broke out in 1932, paving the way for military dictatorship for decades to come. On the whole, Western liberalism appeared to be moribund.

The Third Cycle

The third period of the Westernism-and-Traditionalism cycle began in 1945. This proved to be the greatest turning point in Asian history. Among the many epoch-making milestones of history, no turning point could claim to be its equal in the scope, breadth, depth, and magnitude of change. During World War II, the European colonial powers had to withdraw from large areas of Northeast and Southeast Asia; and Japan, an Asian imperialistic power, moved in to fill in the power vacuum, but only for a short time. Even after the Japanese surrender on August 15, 1945, none of the former colonial powers could survive in Asia. Now all the pent-up emotions in Asia burst into action. The yang forces became ubiquitous. The winds of change sweeping over Asia from then on left no stone unturned.

The progressive development of the bipolar struggle between the United States and the Soviet Union provided Asians, ironically enough, with a good opportunity, probably the best opportunity, to assert their claims. With the urgency of times, the modern Rip Van Winkles of postwar Asia were impatient, anxious to bypass the long historical route of Western progress and jump into what they called modernity. During the years immediately following World War II, both the United States and the Soviet Union presented themselves as models for modernization. A few historical cases may illuminate the situation more clearly. Japan underwent considerable changes. For nearly seven years after her unconditional surrender by accepting the Potsdam Declaration, she was under American occupation. With the aim of building Japan on the American model, the U.S. occupation authorities under General Douglas MacArthur carried out, quite successfully, such laudable reforms as demilitarization, reducing the domination of a few families in industry, commerce, and finance, and land redistribution. Political parties were reorganized, school systems were restructured, and the new constitution of 1947 was promulgated. The American occupation of South Korea was not as well prepared, but even more influential in the long run. Under the direct rule of the American Military Government headed by General John Hodge, a new bureaucracy, a new armed forces, many educational institutions, and business enterprises were born. The American way of life had a deep impact upon the Korean psyche.

On the other hand, equally strong, if not equally lasting, was the Russian influence on the birth of Red China. However great Mao Tse-tung's leadership was, no one can deny the fact that the Soviet Red Army, which had occupied Manchuria, played a major role in the success of Red China. Mao did not forget his indebtedness to the Kremlin. On October 1, 1949, when the Chinese People's Republic was formally proclaimed, what appeared to come into being with extraordinary rapidity was an Asian Soviet Union: government, economy, army, law, education, mass media were all modeled on those of the Soviet Union. Likewise, today's North Korean regime was a brain-child of the Kremlin's from the beginning. During World War II, General T. F. Shytikov, head of Soviet Intelligence in the Siberian region, decided to train Kim Il Sung and his handful of followers who had originally been a guerrilla band in Manchuria. The Red Army brought this group into North Korea, and, with cajolery when needed and with force when necessary, the Russians compelled Koreans to accept Kim's leadership in their zone.

In Southeast Asia, changes were gradual but equally distinct. After the Japanese surrender, Burma, Malaya, South Vietnam, and Indonesia were occupied, at least for a short period, by British forces. The Nationalist Chinese forces moved into North Vietnam to disarm the Japanese forces there. For some time nothing appeared certain. Confusion prevailed. In this chaotic situation, the old dominant class was dying hard. Of course, the traditional ties of family, clanship, and communalism were still strong, but the value of individual abilities began to be recognized. We see a distinct increase of the new breed of leaders who, whatever their social origins had been, were interested in remolding their societies after America, Soviet Russia, or Britain.

The change in the Philippines was smooth. During the war, the exiled government of the Philippines Commonwealth existed in Washington, D.C. When the Republic of the Philippines was inaugurated on July 4, 1946—the anniversary of American Independence—the new constitution was a replica of the U.S. Constitution. The case of Indonesia was somewhat complicated. During the Japanese occupation era, Sukarno and other nationalist leaders cooperated with the Japanese to further nationalist causes; and on August 17, 1945, they swiftly proclaimed their independence with a hastily drafted constitution modeled after the U.S. Constitution. Thus, when Lt. General P. A. Christison led his British soldiers to Indonesia to disarm the Japanese there, the Dutch soldiers who had been detained were released. In the ensuing years a great deal of struggle between the Indonesian nationalists and the Dutch forces went on, until the Hague Agreement of 1949 recognized the sovereignty of Indonesia.

In Burma, the British read the handwriting on the wall and virtually treated the Anti-Fascist People's Freedom League as a *de facto* government as early as 1945. Although

Aung San was assassinated by his political opponents in 1947, Burmese independence was effectuated in 1948 under the leadership of U Nu. Equally smooth was the independence of India. There, the struggle in the immediate postwar years was not between the British and the Indian nationalists, but between the Hindus and the Moslems, eventually producing a Moslem state, Pakistan, in addition to India. Despite the long British rule, the British system was still very much admired in both India and in Pakistan.

The situation in Malaya was quite different, however. Malaya had been divided into nine British protectorates and three crown colonies. During World War II, the Malay People's Anti-Japanese Army fought against Japanese rule, but this paramilitary organization was mainly composed of Chinese inhabitants who dominated it to such an extent that the Malayans rather favored the return of British rule than the power of the Chinese. Therefore, at the time of Malayan independence in 1956, the British left a deep influence upon the country. Even in North Vietnam where Ho Chi Min emerged as the undisputed leader, there was a brief time when the Vietnamese tried to model their new government upon some aspects of the U.S. Constitution. An American OSS team, the Deer Mission, headed by Major Allison K. Thomas, was with Ho and assisted him in drafting the first constitution of North Vietnam.

Of course, it goes without saying that imitating someone else's system is not as easy as it may appear. We, the Asians, could not translate other people's cultures, institutions, social norms, and ways of life as was initially expected. Political institutions could be imitated on paper, but making them actually work was an entirely different matter. Western economic systems without related economic ethics became defunct. In spite of the many difficulties arising from both within and without, what the Asian nations have thus far achieved has been laudable; but at the same time, we have to admit that many things also went dreadfully wrong. The fruits of modernization all too often benefited only a small ruling minority. The masses were forcibly mobilized without receiving just compensation; consequently democracy eroded rapidly.

In this situation, starting from about the mid-1950s, Westernism was again discredited, distrusted, and criticized. Intellectual and political leaders began to voice disillusionment with the American type of democracy. The yin phase began. Criticisms of Western democracy varied. Some said it was too individualistic. Others said it was too mechanistic to be adaptable to Asian societies. By the same token, Communism was too contrary to Asian tradition to be transplanted. At this crossroads, most of the non-Communist Asian states produced variant versions of democracy, largely based upon their respective national traditions.

Sukarno's Guided Democracy in Indonesia was a typical example. Sukarno's idea of national unity was rather simple—the people should follow one leader, for democracy without leadership could degenerate into mass rule. Defining his concept of Guided Democracy, Sukarno said that the law of *musjawarah* (discussion) and *mufakat* (agreement) in accordance with Indonesian tradition must be essential; but once decided, no one was to argue against it. There must be only action, action which would be directed by one leader.

U Nu of Burma produced the idea of the Religious State on the basis of Burmese national tradition. In his speech to the third All Burma Congress in 1958, U Nu said that capitalist democracy was not suitable for Burma because the capitalists wanted profit and unavoidably exploited the masses. On the other hand, he pointed out that Marxism was too dogmatic to be applicable to his country. What U Nu suggested was the synthesis of both democracy and Communism into the Burmese tradition of religion: 1) Lord Buddha's mercy in politics as a guiding moral foundation; 2) no use of force and arms, either domestically or internationally; and 3) the construction of a socialist state with Buddhism as its unifying spiritual force.

Less philosophical and even more confusing was Ngo

Dinh Diem's Personalism. It was an eclectic mixture of French existentialism, Confucian ethics, and Catholicism. With his mandarin background and humanistic learning, Diem conceived of the state as an organ to create an environment for individuals to perfect their personalities. In Korea, Syngman Rhee at one time talked about Il-Min Chui (one people's democracy), but his ideas remained ambiguous. In Pakistan, Ayub Kahn advocated the True Democracy, with his ideas largely remaining in crude forms.

On the whole, in spite of the expansive rhetoric, Asiatic democracies lacked pragmatic and scientific self-searching. Nor were they rationally systematized. They were merely useful tools for the existing rulers, and without universality they could not survive. Suffice it to say that these first generation leaders, notwithstanding their honesty and dedication, failed to produce new social and political ideologies to supplant the ideals of Western democracy. The road for the second wave of political revolution was wide open.

The Fourth Cycle

The fourth period of the Westernism-and-Traditionalism cycle according to this study began in the early 1960s. By this time most Asians were deeply frustrated. We experienced an anticlimax following the "revolution of expectation." But having had little experience in political acculturation, interest articulation, and interest aggregation, the common people had no way to express their frustration. Only students and urban workers displayed their disgruntlement by staging demonstrations and riots, but such mass actions merely made the leaders in power more hardened and callous. Elections were rigged, and political oppression escalated. Against this dismal background the military stepped in.

After overthrowing the first generation of leadership in the 1960s, the military revolutionaries began carrying out sweeping changes in all areas of life. With their experience in management learned in the armed forces, they skillfully

dealt with the daily problems of government. Strong in social consciousness, they carried out many laudable reforms
in social welfare, land reforms, industrialization, and social
restratification.

But as time went by, it became increasingly clear that
overthrowing a government was much easier than managing it effectively. However pure and honest had been their
original motives, the military leaders who overthrew the
existing lawful governments by means of violence were
after all human beings, always susceptible to the innate
weaknesses of man—weaknesses such as vanity and arro-
gance. As Lord Acton's dictum says, "Power corrupts and
absolute power corrupts absolutely." Injustice, more than
anything else, has permeated all levels of society, and many
governments of Asia have become unduly oppressive and
repressive. Human rights have been trampled down. At the
moment, the political power of these second generation
leaders is so efficiently, so scientifically organized that any
mass protest against them appears to be impossible. Yet
suppression alone is not enough to maintain the status quo.
In what direction should we Asians now move?

3. PRESENT OPTION: ARCHAISM OR FUTURISM?

Except for a few Communist states still clinging to idiosyn-
cratic dogmatism, practically all the Asian nations, including Japan, have lost their direction. Where can we find a
new breakthrough at this time of great confusion? Are we to
let ourselves drift like floating flowers in the tide of time?
Adrift in the surging waves which roar endlessly, without
any knowledge of our future direction, we are insecure and
fearful. The future has become a horrible source of anxiety,
deeper in degree than ever before. With the speed of historical change today moving over a hundred times faster than
in the past, we are perplexed, dismayed, and disheartened.

Suggested remedies range over a wide spectrum from the
extreme left to the extreme right, with all sorts of opinions
in between. Many think that we must strive for a more

thoroughgoing modernization, modeling our institutions and modes of living more completely after the West. Left-wing futurism vehemently advocates that in view of the failure of capitalistic democracy in Asia, we must find a new direction in Communism, which claims to be marching in step with the times. After Indo-China succumbed to Communism, many people began to doubt the survival of non-Communist nations in Asia.

But at the moment another school of thought which dominates the climate of opinion in Asia insists that what we Asians have to do most urgently and imperatively is to rediscover, retrieve, and regain our self-identity and national character, which was lost in our haste to Westernize. Futurism, be it capitalistic or Communistic, moves forward by negating the past, thereby unintentionally negating self-identity. To borrow other people's cultural heritage without a clear national consciousness accompanying it is analagous to a young girl who, with no sense of individual identity, follows the passing fads of the changing times endlessly, wearing a mini-skirt one day and a maxi-skirt the next.

In terms of the Westernism-and-Traditionalism cycle discussed in this study, we are now living in the yin phase of the fourth period. This may sound as though Asia is trapped by the deterministic yin-yang cycle, circling around the fatalistic wheel endlessly and moving nowhere. But the opposite is more true. By looking beyond the descriptive aspects of the surface phenomena, we find that these cycles have been in fact spirals chained to a greater linear progression of historical time which makes a discernible ascending movement.

Taking the four yin phases, for instance, from each period we discussed, we see an interesting pattern of Asian intellectual growth. The first yin phase was the blind reaction of ultraconservatism against Westernization. In it we found a strong strain of reactionism. Compared to this, the second yin phase was dominated by moderation which advocated gradual changes. The third yin phase sought the creation of new Asian ideologies. Now the fourth yin phase, which began at the beginning of the 1970s, advocates the rediscovery of national self-identity without blindly negating Western thought. I have a hunch that the forces of continuity will hold the lead for many years to come.

A Korean newspaper editorial laments the present situation of Asia in a candid and frank tone, saying: "Our intellectual history of the postwar age has been an age of self-abnegation under the tidal challenge of Westernism. But now, even the exogenous forces of an international trend call us to turn to things of our own. Not only politically, but also intellectually, we must reestablish our national subjecthood."[7] An Asian scholarly journal prefaces its inaugural number with the following remarks: "Tradition is the very source of creation and the material cause for new forms, and any creation without tradition is comparable to a tree with no roots."[8]

Speaking purely theoretically, we can take this resurgence of traditionalism in the fourth period of this study as a broad Asian renaissance which, by grafting Western heritage upon traditional foundations, wants to create something new and more glorious. Unlike the previous nativistic reactions against hasty Westernization, it is not mere cultural chauvinism. It goes beyond and above blind nativism. In brief, as previously observed, it is an effort to rediscover self-identity, both individually and nationally.

Today more Asian nations stress the importance of educating youth in their national tradition. In India, in Malaysia, and, to a certain extent, in the Philippines, more time is allotted in school for students to study their respective languages, and naturally less time for English. National history and culture are emphasized far more. In Iran, the teaching of the Koran on the elementary level has been reemphasized. Archaeologists are busy digging up graves to discover artifacts of their forefathers, artifacts which embody the spiritual source of their tradition.

Already, although admittedly it is still too early to pass judgment on their results, some tangible fruits have been born of this trend. The revival of the past cultural heritages does not necessarily mean a movement to the bygone days; on the contrary, the reverse is true. By mixing the elements of the past and those of the present, cultural creativity becomes revitalized, recharged, and reactivated.

In the visual arts, the possibility of making new breakthroughs in forms, styles, and techniques can be limitless. Unpretentious, tranquill, and reticent in beauty, Oriental painting, for instance, expresses deep humane feelings—feelings which, when mixed with the techniques of Western painting, can become a new source of creativity. The creative fusion of Oriental artistic elements and Western techniques in sculpture, ceramics, embroidery, and lacquer may open new frontiers in aesthetics. In medicine, acupuncture has performed some wonders. In philosophy, the Oriental intuitive approach to life may open many new insights, hereunto hidden to the analytical minds of the West. In ethics, our traditional humaneness in social relations can make positive contributions to the rehumanization of the modern life. Already, definite progress has been made in placing the meeting of East and West on an equal footing.

Probably, and perhaps rightly, the Chinese Cultural Revolution can be reinterpreted in terms of this forward-looking archaism. The Red Guard phase of the Cultural Revolution was essentially political rather than cultural, but we know that it was also an attempt to resuscitate Maoism in the minds of the Chinese who, after nearly two decades under the Red regime, had begun to take Maoistic ideals rather casually. By launching a full-fledged attack upon Confucianism, Mao Tse-tung endeavored to eradicate the Chinese orthodox tradition and to replace it with his own ideology before his death. Futuristic as it appears, this movement was nevertheless anachronistic, for Maoism had

drawn its sources from more Chinese heterodoxical tradition than Marxism itself.

Ironically enough, the revival of Maoism will also revive
many Chinese heterodoxical traditions. In its own way, the
anti-Confucian movement of Red China is in fact a form of
archaism. Likewise, in North Korea, a similar movement to
return to Korean tradition began in the name of rediscovering *juche* (national subjecthood). Caught in the middle of
the Sino-Soviet conflict, Kim Il Sung steered an independent course by keeping his nation an equal distance from
Peking and Moscow. On the pretext of reviving national
subjecthood, Kim intensified his own personality cult,
thereby strengthening his dictatorship in the face of the
winds of change sweeping all over Asia.

On the whole, in the political realm, this movement to
return to traditionalism has become a modern trend. Western democracy is no longer sacrosanct among non-Communist Asian nations. The Western democratic power
mechanism has had only limited success, for it had been
basically aimed at stabilizing society and not at mobilizing
people for progress. In some cases, the parliamentary system of the Western type, being so cumbersome and slow in
action, was too inflexible to keep pace with the rapidly
changing political situation in Asia. Also, the passing of the
cold war frame of reference made the Asian leaders tense,
thus encouraging them to tighten their political control internally.

As a matter of fact, the form of government borrowed
from the West has invariably produced many adverse effects upon Asian society. According to A. F. K. Organski,
"The Western nations have attained their present state of
political maturity in a long historical course through four
stages: first, the stage of the politics of national unification;
second, the stage of the politics of industrialization; third,
the stage of the politics of national welfare; and fourth, the
present stage of the politics of abundance."[9]

If Organski's theory of political development, despite its

clumsy artificiality, contains some truth, most Asian nations, at the time of their national independence, adopted the highly developed government forms of the third stage. Consequently, the gap between political structure and social reality could not be bridged as originally envisaged. In retrospect, one may well contend that the Asian nations could have done better had they adopted stronger forms of government from the beginning. In any event, the triple tasks of national unification, industrialization, and social welfare, with scant capital and technological skill, could not be carried out simultaneously.

In reality, many Asian nations became bogged down in the first, the primary task of national unification. Except for Korea, China, Japan, and Thailand, most Asian nations had no clear-cut collective consciousness of national unity. An Indonesian foreign minister lamented the sad reality, saying, "We were only united against the Dutch. After that we are island against island, province again province, intellectual against intellectual, religion against religion."[10] Ruper Emerson's phrase, "not yet nations in being but only in hope," was a truism.[11]

Yet I personally think that the real cause of the problems in post-independence Asia was not so much one of form as the lack of spirit which could sustain superstructures. For instance, the legislative organ, often filled by political adventurers, never enjoyed the prestige of the parliament in the West. As a result it was soon overshadowed by the executive branch which also reduced the judiciary to its rubber stamp. Nevertheless, people had no spirits to resist against such trends. Though political parties had good formal structures, no spirit of compromise—an essential quality of democracy—worked within the party to make the party system productive. In the economic realm, the policies of industrialization made business firms subservient to political power. Moreover, the shortage of trained personnel was most acute, for only a small fragment of the populace in each country had even a secondary school level education. The government of each country, ambitious but with little experience in carrying out innovative plans, had meager sources of income; nor was there a viable middle class to bear the burden.

Dismayed by the frustrating problems arising from their efforts at modernization, coupled with the Nixon Shock, the Dollar Shock, and the Oil Shock, the smaller non-Communist Asian nations sought to establish a sense of national security by tightening political control. Old constitutions which had been patterned after Western models were scrapped, and a new constitutions, with the familar features of traditional autocracy, replaced them. Invariably the executive branch of government has become almost omnipotent, with presidential powers virtually unlimited and unchecked. All too often this increasing political control is justified in the name of "national self-identity," emphasizing that every nation should follow different paths to attain democracy.

Summing up, we see that the *Zeitgeist* of today's Asia is the spiritual outcry of people to revive traditional heritages in the place of hasty Westernization; but this outcry, like Janus, has two faces, one good and one bad. The revival of archaic traditions can provide us with a new source of creativity, creativity which may push us toward a brighter future; yet at the same time it has inherent limitations which will eventually choke us to death.

I personally see in archaism more dangers than possibilities. With no sense of disparaging the apparent merits of the revival of traditional heritages, I, as a historian, must warn of its dangers in a few categories.

First, if carried to the extreme this tendency becomes utterly anachronistic, eventually stagnating and strangulating our social and cultural growth. A classic example of this retrogressive renaissance is found in the Ming archaism of China. As we know well, the Ming Dynasty, established in the fourteenth century, was a result of Chinese reaction against the foreign Mongol rule. Naturally the cultural policy of the Ming was to extirpate foreign elements from the Chinese society, and to revive the old heritages of the Han Dynasty and the Tang Dynasty. In the end, ironically enough, this effort proved to be too successful to be really successful. With the old social structures, norms, mores, political organizations, and philosophical thoughts of the Han and the Tang revived in reality, the Ming Dynasty turned the clock backward a few hundred years, at the precise time when the West was busy making the transformation that gave birth to modernity.

Paradoxically enough, the Western Renaissance was productive, mainly because of its failure to revive the Greco-Roman heritage in its original form. Renaissance painters and sculptors tried to copy the ancient masterpieces, but in so doing, by fusing the old forms and styles of the Greco-Romans into what they had already known during the Middle Ages, they produced a new cultural tradition, novel and noble. If we are to take a lesson from history, our present efforts to revive our traditional heritages should be forward-looking rather than nostalgic.

Second, we must not fall into the pitfall of cultural chauvinism. A typical historical example of cultural chauvinism and its lethal effects can be found in the revival of Slavism in nineteenth-century Russia. As a spiritual reaction against the hasty Westernization policies of Peter and Catherine, the Russian intelligentsia of the post-Napoleonic era, steeped in German romanticism, advocated the resurrection of the "Russian soul" which, in their view, had become moribund in the tidal challenge of Westernism.

Increasingly opposed to the secular, materialistic, and sensual culture of the West, they rediscovered Slavism in the three pillars of the Russian traditions; namely, *narodinik* (people), benevolent autocracy, and the Orthodox Church.[12] With firm faith in the superiority of Slavism over and against Westernism, the Russian intelligentsia went directly to the people to awaken them in the traditional heritage by popularizing their ideas and ideals. But by becoming xenophobic to the extent of slandering Western democracy and praising the traditional Russian autocracy, they unwittingly paved the way for the rise of Bolshevik totalitarianism.

Third, we must guard against the danger of making the present Asian renaissance movement a political tool of the ruling elite. A typical example of this danger was the revival of the Japanese-Soul Movement in prewar Japan. It began in Japan in the late 1920s, mostly inspired by the lunatic intellectuals such as Kita Ikki who had been disillusioned by Western thought, particularly in the wake of the failure of the party government. They advocated, for instance, the wiping out of whatever democratic processes still remained in Japanese politics for the sake of the revival of Japanese tradition and outlined a program of action in terms of the suspension of constitution, the limitation of private property, and the strengthening of the *kokutai* (a mysterious concept of Japanese nationhood) through emperor worship.

Very soon this intellectual movement was utilized by the rising militarists in their justification of military dictatorship. In the end, by reviving the old ghosts of Shintoism and emperor worship, Japanese militarists led the nation into the abyss of total destruction in World War II. Evidently the search for national self-identity, can, when directed by politicans, be used for wrong political motives.

Besides these unhappy historical precedents, many adverse effects of traditionalism can be observed in today's Asia. In many countries individual rights have been suspended, citizens are liable for arrest and trial by special military courts, the press has been suppressed, and political opposition is silenced by torture and assassination. The theorum that anyone who does not learn from history will surely repeat historical mistakes is proving itself in today's Asia.

All in all, suffice it to say that the forward-looking archaism has shown its limitations. Probably a swing to the past is a necessary course that every historical development takes, but the swing to traditionalism has already proven to be far from adequate to guide the future destiny of Asians. What then is a better course? Let us now examine the second option before us, namely, the option of futurism.

Observing the dilemma of archaism which has become increasingly aggravated, many Asian intellectuals suggest another direction for us. This school of thought says that up until now the Asians, while over-decorating the facade of modern institutions that they have borrowed from the West, have not really tried to provide them with a spiritual milieu that would enable them to take root in Asian cultural soil. Instead of reviving our traditional heritages, which failed to give birth to modernity, what we really have to do is move forward with drastic and wholesale Westernization.

This school points out that we Asians, in spite of our continuous efforts to modernize our societies, have not really tried all-out Westernization. What we have done so far has in fact been to learn from Western technology and science while excluding other spiritual values. But inasmuch as a civilization is likened to an organic life with its myriad of variant components, we cannot choose in the process of cultural borrowing some desirable elements and exclude undesirable elements. Piecemeal Westernization of the late Ch'ing era in China, for instance, was neither workable nor productive. That being the case, what we must do most urgently is to launch a thoroughgoing Westernization in all realms of life, both physical and spiritual.

The failure of our efforts to democratize our political structures—a most conspicuous example of the "failure" of modernization—was not because of the unsuitability of our cultural soil for Western democracy, but because of our half-hearted efforts to learn the spiritual values underlying it. Democracy and the spirit of freedom are inseparable, for democratic institutions nurture and are being nurtured by human freedom. But our governments, despite their democratic structures based upon the principles of the separation of powers and of the checks and balances among them, have not really exerted all-out efforts to engender free speech and free press. Contrary to the constitutional guarantee, human rights have been transgressed, violated, and trampled down by the ever-growing, almost omnipotent power of the government. All too often humble people are arrested, tortured, and imprisoned without due process of law. Thus according to this futuristic school, we must give a new thrust to the democratization of our society on the Western model. What then is the present condition of Western civilization? Is it still viable, virile, and dynamic enough to serve as our future model?

Opinions about the present condition of Western civilization, however, vary greatly, ranging from extreme optimism to extreme pessimism. Optimists, still clinging to the cult of Progress, depict the future of the West with highly imaginative rosy pictures. In line with the secular millenia predicted by Comte, Spencer, and Bellamy, Daniel Bell calls today's West "the postindustrial society" in which consumption has become a new virtue. Peter Drucker thinks that today's West is in an age of "discontinuity" which heralds a new and more glorious era. Kenneth Boulding, a cautious optimist, concludes by saying, "In spite of the dangers, it is a wonderful age to live in, and I would not wish to be born in any other time."[13]

The advanced societies of the West, viewed superficially, continue to make progress in science and technology, producing opulence which defies the imagination. In some countries like the United States spending has almost become a virtue, with avaricious consumption becoming a new habit of life even among the working people. Even medieval lords did not enjoy the living standard of the average Western man today.

But on the other hand, pessimists are equally vociferous. Ruminating upon the Cassandra-like forebodings of Schopenhauer, Nietzsche, and Spengler, they point out the innumerable symptoms of sickness in the West. John H. Hallowell, for example, writes:

> It requires no great seer or prophet to discern today the signs of decadence that are everywhere manifest. Only the most stubborn and obtuse would venture optimistic predictions for the future of the world and its civilization. The complacent optimism of the last century has given way to a deep-rooted despair and men everywhere are gripped by fear and insecurity. Anxiety gnaws at their vitals.[14]

To evaluate the relative merits and demerits of these two diametrically opposed schools is beyond the scope of this work. Numerous books on this subject are available. Yet I personally feel that of the two schools of thought, pessimism dominates the general climate of opinion among Western intellectuals today. In the West, something is wrong, dreadfully wrong. The optimistic dreams of the nineteenth century prophets are shattered.

The "progress" that Western man has so proudly made over the centuries since the Renaissance has, to his dismay, turned against him: modern science threatens his very existence, advanced technology enslaves him, efficiency produces impersonalization among human beings, massive organizations breed alienation, and peace movements procreate wars. As C. Virgil Gheorghiu laments, today's West seems to be in its "twenty-fifth hour," the hour from which the clock cannot turn back to normalcy.

In the advanced societies of the West, mega-machines, scientific principles, and many other nonhuman forces dominate human life. Not being free, the Western man can be less and less ethical in taking responsibility for his actions. With all due respect, I must say that today's average Western man is quite mixed up. Superficially, he is cheerful, friendly, outgoing, and even to some extent capricious. But deep in his psychic substrata he seems to suffer from fear and anxiety, which makes him irritable, grumpy, frenzied, and to a large extent neurotic. It is as difficult for Asians to understand the dual personality of the Western man as it is for Westerners to understand Asians.

All I mean to say at this point is that despite the dazzling material affluence of the West, the Western way of life can no longer be a model for future Asian societies. Thinking that blindly adopting the Western model will enable us to climb the rainbow bridge to utopia will merely lead us to fantasy. Figuratively speaking, the fruits of the tree (Western civilization) are still growing and ripening, but hidden beneath the surface, the roots are decaying. I may touch upon the major causes of the "decline of the West" in some other parts of this work, but at any rate the Western model has become outdated.

To those Asians who have become disillusioned with the Western model, Communism may appear to be an alternative to despair. Unlike the loose liberal doctrines of Western democracy, Marxism offers programs of action for change and claims to provide solutions to every conceivable problem arising in the course of modernization.

In his *Asia Awakes*, Dick Wilson breaks down the appeal of Communism in Asia into the following categories: First, intellectually it meets the need for a cosmic explanation based on scientific reasoning. Second, politically it offers a model for change, for reform, for revolution, and for nation-building by the tight, cohesive political means of mass mobilization. Third, emotionally "its adherents are made to feel part of a vast and universal movement, flowing with the mainstream of history, informed with optimism and idealism." And fourth, historically the Soviet Government was sympathetic toward Asian nationalist movements as early as 1919, as was shown with the Karakhan Manifesto.[15]

Notwithstanding the fact that Marxism was born in Western industrial society as an attempt to solve the complex socio-economic problems arising from industrialization, it found fertile ground in the agrarian societies of

Asia, largely because of conditions uniquely Asian. For instance, the Chinese people traditionally adhered to a comprehensive *Weltanshauung*, such as Confucianism or Taoism, in their life; and as these traditional doctrines eroded so rapidly, they were seeking other ideological foundations to stand on. Also, in the absence of a bourgeoisie, most Asian people had no clear concept of the private possession of property, with its rights and duties well defined in a code of behavior, and therefore communal ownership of land was less feared. Likewise, with little experience in living under a democratic government, political centralization was less objectionable to Asians than to people in the West.

In retrospect, we see that by 1949, when Communist governments were firmly established in mainland China, northern Korea, and North Vietnam, with Communist Parties in other Asian nations quite actively engaged in subversive actions, many people in the East and in the West were apprehensive, fearing the total Sovietization of Asia. The domino theory was widely accepted. The Japanese Communist Party in 1949 received nearly 10 percent of the total votes in the election; in the Philippines, the Huks became ebullient; in Malaya, the Communist-controlled Malayan National Liberation Army fought against the British; in Laos, the Pathet Lao was in its gestation period; and in Indonesia, Sukarno had to vie with the Indonesian Communist Party. In a poem of Iqbal, the spiritual father of Pakistan, some Asian leaders' feelings toward the Soviet model were summarized:

> It comes to me, observing how our sovereign states proceed,
> That not without utility was Russia's headlong speed.

However, now in the 1970s, the situation has changed somewhat. Although the Communist threat against non-Communist nations in Asia has considerably increased in the aftermath of the downfall of South Vietnam, Cambodia, and Laos, some hopeful signs are equally evident. The

menace of North Korea is less real than apparent; the Huks
in the Philippines no longer possess the power to destroy
the government; the Indonesian Communist Party has not
recovered from the serious setback suffered at its premature
coup attempt of 1965; and in Burma, Communism as a potent political force is not so menacing as it used to be. Only
in Thailand and in Malaysia have Communist guerrilla
forces become more active in recent years. But without military aid from the Communist superpowers, the Soviet
Union and Red China, the Communist forces presently
operating within these countries may not be able to overthrow the legitimate governments.

In spite of some obvious dangers still existing, the overall
picture in Asia has improved considerably. Fewer people
any longer take the domino theory seriously. Especially
after the beginning of détente between the United States
and Red China and the intensification of the Sino-Soviet
dispute, Communist expansion in Asia has shown some of
its limits. How has this situation developed? A few reasons
may account for this change.

First, the Asians have observed the inherent
contradictions—"antagonistic contradictions"—of the
Soviet system. This is to say that when Communism was
first introduced to Asia, it was a fresh idea untried in historical time; but now the Communist system, with a history of
a half-century, has lost its fresh appeal. Especially during
the de-Stalinization era, Khruschev and others exposed
much of the inhumane brutality and terrorism of the Stalin
regime. The whole Soviet Union has now become an *Animal
Farm*, as depicted by George Orwell, or at best the *New
Class* society that Milovan Djilas so abhorred.

Second, we have seen clearly the dissension among the
Communist countries themselves. The brutality demonstrated by the Soviet Army in suppressing the freedom
movements in Hungary and Poland in 1956, and again in
Czechoslovakia in 1968, was appalling; but above all, the
progressive development of the Sino-Soviet conflict has

produced multiple effects upon the Asian psyche. The reasons behind this struggle, fast becoming a powder-keg in Northeast Asia, are too numerous to be listed here. When Red China was developing the atomic bomb with the help of U.S.-trained scientists like Tsien Hsue-shen, the Kremlin refused to supply information. The coexistence policy of Khruschev ran counter to Mao Tse-tung's theory of world revolution. So in August 1960 Moscow recalled 10,800 of its technicians who had been helping Red China. In addition to these points of contention, racial feeling and increasing border disputes have had serious effects upon the split between these two Communist giants.

In this situation, the Asian Communist Parties had to take sides, either backing the Soviet Union or Red China, and they have been in a quandary, not knowing what to do. The Japanese Communist party, after a period of indecision, concluded that neither direction was satisfactory and decided to remain independent; the result was that it found its influence was eroding. The Sino-Soviet dispute, more than anything else, has demoralized the Asian Communist movements in many countries.

Third, as time goes by, the basic Maoist formula for modernization becomes increasingly unacceptable to Asian minds. With its inhumane methods of mass mobilization, Red China has carried out successive economic plans, but its gross national product is still only slightly over one-third of Japan's and one-tenth of the United States's. She still has a long way to go before becoming a truly industrialized country. And yet the price the people have had to pay for the changes is exorbitant. Mao became deified and Maoism sanctified. No individual freedom exists in Red China. The power struggle after Mao's death has been a bloody confrontation between the moderates and the radicals.

Fourth, the North Korean model appears to be even less viable. The Pyongyang regime was the brain-child of the Kremlin, having had its inception in Siberia under the guidance of Soviet intelligence organizations. During the

Korean War, Kim Il Sung survived the retaliation of the Republic of Korea Army only through Red Chinese intervention. As the Sino-Soviet dispute worsened in the post-Korean War era, Kim Il Sung, after wobbling for some years, formulated an independent line in the name of *juche*, the spirit of national identity; but his new policy is in the main a smoke-screen to justify his personality cult. Now he is a living god, and there is no other ideology in North Korea except that of Kim's *juche*. Regardless of who succeeds Kim, North Korean leadership may become extremely poor in quality, for he has successively, through the years, exterminated the South Korean Communist faction, the *Yenan* faction, and the Soviet faction.

I cannot, of course, disregard the role that accidents play in human history. In view of the situation in Europe today, in which the Communist Party is suddenly on the ascendancy in Portugal, Spain, and Italy, many Asian nations, suffering more serious economic woes, cannot remain free from the danger of Communist takeover. But I firmly believe that most Asian nations will not be transformed into Communist states peacefully on their own initiative, unless they are compelled to do so by unavoidable historical accidents. To think of Communism as a model for the future is in itself an anachronistic view of today's Asia.

2

Christianity and Historical Transfiguration

On the whole, today's Asia is at a crossroads and is in a transitional dilemma, with the forces of futurism and traditionalism equally viable and strong. Asia is moving forward and moving backward simultaneously. It is changing and yet remains changeless; it is converging and diverging, shrinking and expanding, and conglomerating and fragmentalizing concomitantly. It is modernizing and traditionalizing at the same time in the same time-spatial dimension. In other words, Asia is experiencing a revolution leading nowhere.

What we need most urgently and most imperatively is not a movement on the horizontal plane, moving to and fro like a pendulum between modernization and traditionalization, but a great vertical leap—an *Aufheben*—in order to create a new civilization which is neither of the East nor of the West. Philosophers call this jump a dialectical change, a change which is brought about by the synthesis of thesis and antithesis. Better still, the Bible calls it "transfiguration," as seen in the resurrected life of Jesus Christ—life both physical and spiritual transcending both in an entirely new form. Speaking in secularized terms, our goal hereafter must be to achieve a new transfiguration by a creative synthesis of the best elements of both the East and of the West.

1. CAUSAL FACTORS OF HISTORICAL PROGRESS

We have come to a new dimension in our discussion, a new dimension in dealing with a more fundamental question in historical thinking. What are the major causal factors which bring forth progress in human history? How can we make an *Aufheben* possible by synthesizing all the contradictory phenomena circulating throughout today's Asia? Since these questions lie deeper than the surface phenomena that empirical historians can analyze, they require philosophical introspection. This point is the meeting ground of history and philosophy, but the results of speculative historical thought thus far undertaken have been far from satisfactory. Theories, hypotheses, and speculative ideas abound; but unlike natural science, historical postulates cannot be empirically proven or disproven. We can "remember" historical events, but cannot "reconstruct" them as they actually happened.

Historians deal with human events. Natural events, although not entirely excluded from historical thinking, come to the attention of historians only in terms of their connection with human life. This is to say that though the world in which we live is one inseparable unit, we have to divide it into two separate realms, the natural and historical, if we are to understand the uniqueness of the historical world. Whereas nature moves in accordance with certain fixed laws comprehensive to us through reasoning and scientific observation, human events cannot be scrutinized with the same precision because of their essential difference from natural phenomena.

Unlike natural events, human affairs are motivated by diversified, complex human desires which cannot be quantitatively reduced into a few exhaustive units or categories. The life of man changes constantly and continuously in time and in place, for it is not only something which *is*, but also something which is *becoming*. Man is influenced by the situation in which he finds himself, but by the same token, he creates a new situation, too. As he changes continually, his multifarious desires likewise change, making every individual event unique in itself. Being unique, a human event cannot recur in historical time.

Also troublesome to historical thinkers is the problem of evaluating historical events. Because they are motivated by human will, all historical events have moral implications. Suppose, for instance, historians are to evaluate a labor strike. A historian sympathetic to the working class may praise it, while another historian who sides with the capitalists may denounce it. Here exists the danger of making biased judgments on historical events. After all, historians as human beings can hardly transcend the prejudices that stem from their individual backgrounds.

Because of these factors, plus many more complicated epistemological problems involving historical thinking, it is almost impossible to deduce "historical laws" in the same manner as natural scientists discover natural laws. The historical evidences available for us are, oddly enough, too many and too few. In the first place, within the last century, overwhelming quantities of historical materials have been found in archives, private and public; and in our day, with the development of the computer and microfilms, both written and visual materials have become nightmarishly abundant. But at the same time, historical data are, despite their abundance, not enough with which to construct historical laws.

To historians, the history of mankind as we know it today is only a fragment of man's experiences on earth. We do not know enough about the dreams of man played on the time-spatial dimension, not enough to be able to arrange them into that comprehensive arrangement of regularities, uniformities, and repetitions which we call "laws." Fragmented stone implements and human skeletons from the old stone ages do not give sufficient evidence as to how people lived and what they believed in. Therefore, scepticism abounds in historical thought.

Yet we cannot stand still. To sit idly by and give unconditional support to scepticism leads us nowhere. While today's historians lapse in intellectual languor by merely doing nothing but describing historical facts as they oc- cured, sociologists economists, psychologists, an- thropologists, and political scientists have discovered many uniformities in human conduct in their respective fields, almost analogous to what natural scientists achieved in the eighteenth century. In *A Study of History*, Arnold Toynbee cautiously calls for our attention to the fact that historians too can find some regularities in human affairs.[1]

Statistical studies show us consumer behavior, trade cy- cles, crime rates, cases of suicide, and divorce rates which can be reduced into some uniform patterns. There are some human psychic patterns common to every individual. View- ing human events over a long time span, historians can find some war-and-peace cycles and cycles in the rise and fall of civilizations.

Therefore, bold meta-historians have been interested in finding sets of historical uniformities, if not laws; and to- day, with the darkening shadows of eschatological symptoms spreading throughout the globe, the number of such speculators has increased. To recite and ruminate upon their already well-known hypotheses lies beyond the range of this work. One theme, however, worth tracing is their theories concerning the primary causal factors of his- torical progress.

In ancient times the question of causal factors in historical progress did not trouble speculative minds for the simple reason that men, believing in the working of deities in human affairs, did not ask such questions. History and myths, human events and deistic actions were inexplicably intertwined, and there existed no way, nor reason, to dif- ferentiate between these two realms. The one common de- nominator underlying the attitudes of all ancient peoples toward history was determinism, a belief that human soci- ety changed endlessly in cyclic forms, as nature changed in time in cyclic movements. Changes in human life, just as in nature, were inevitable; but in the course of time, history returned to the original alpha point from which it had started.

The historicity of the ancient Indians is a case in point. In the Indian mind, both nature and history were one cosmological continuum, inseparable and undistinguishable. Without clear historical consciousness, they believed that changes in both nature and in human society follow the same cosmic process. Therefore, if we are to know the Indian view of history, we must first understand their ancient cosmology.

Like most other ancient peoples, the ancient Dravidians inhabiting the Indus valley and the early Aryans who came into the valley from the north about two millenia B.C. were both nature worshipers. Natural forces were deified and worshiped. As more speculative philosophies developed, however, Hinduism incorporated the many local deities into a more sophisticated cosmological system. The Vedic gods—Indra, Mitra, Varuna, and millions of others—came to be dominated by the trinity—Brahman (Creator), Vishnu (Preserver), and Siva (Destroyer). Through the cosmic times such as Yuga, Mahayuga, and Kalpha, these supreme gods created, destroyed, and recreated the universe repeatedly in eternity. The human being, an insignificant part of this Cosmos, is chained to the eternal cycles of reincarnation.

And then, later, Hinduism has come to believe in a pseudo-monism. This is to say that more sophisticated Hindus believe that there is only one god, Brahman, who dominates the universe. However, unlike Jehovah of the Old Testament, Brahman is not a personal god who has aims, goals, and plans in running the universe. Nor can he listen to our prayer. Rather, this Supreme Self is believed to be "unlimited, unborn, not to be reasoned about, not to be conceived" (Rig Veda VI, 17). If we say that the Absolute has love, we would have to assume that he has something antithetical to love within himself. If we can describe his attributes in limited human terms, he can no longer be the Unlimited Absolute.

But by delving one step deeper we find in the Vedas that Brahman is not the Ultimate Reality of the universe. In the deepest place of Hindu thought lies the concept of *Rita*—the universal and eternal cosmic law—which created everything, including Brahman. Rig Veda X, 129 says the following:

> Non-being then existed not nor being;
> There was no air, nor sky that is beyond it.
> What was concealed? Wherein? In whose protection?
> Creative force was there, and fertile power:
> Below was energy, above was impulse.

Rig Veda IV, 23, 8 says: "Eternal law [*Rita*] hath ı od that strengthens, thought of eternal law moves transgressions." "The Creation Hymn" found in Rig Veda X, 190 also says: "From Fervour kindled to its height Eternal Law and Truth were born." *Rita* is no deity, nor is it a spirit. It has no aim, nor purpose. Nor do we find that it is a blind will. *Rita* is believed to be a creative force, a potential power, which represents the unity and rightness (not righteousness) underlying the orderliness of the universe. It cannot be described in human terms, for anything definable in our language cannot be the Ultimate Reality.

In summary it may suffice to say that the fundamental belief underlying the Indian cosmology is nondeistic. In spite of so many gods praised and talked about in the Vedas, Hinduism is basically agnostic. Instead of believing in a personal God who created and preserves the universe and the human world, Hindus believe in the existence of a cosmic force or a universal principle from which all beings, including gods, have originated. Even gods have to obey the power of this cosmic force, especially when it expresses itself in the form of *dharma* (law).

Man as a part of this grand-scaled cosmic process has no freedom. He has no power to choose his course of life. Chained by *karma* (fate) he lives in *maya* (illusion). Therefore, man's final goal in Hinduism is to liberate himself from the world of phenomena and become united with Brahman, the cosmic Supreme Self. This is *moksa* (salvation). Viewed in this light, history has no meaning, because history and nature in the grand cosmic process are one inseparable whole. Nature, gods, and man are conglomerated into one cosmic unit.

Nor does Buddhism, in spite of its many novel and noble doctrines, basically differ from Hinduism in historical thought. Although Buddha stood against some Vedantic teachings such as the concept of the caste system, he, according to William Theodore DeBary, took an agnostic position with regard to the existence of God and based his world-views upon the Hinduistic cosmology.[2] This is to say that Buddha, too, based his teachings of "the Four Noble Truths of Sorrow," "the Noble Eightfold Path," "the Five Precepts," and "the Middle Way" upon the Hinduistic beliefs such as karma, dharma, moksa, and nirvana. Here again, we see no birth of "historical consciousness." Since history is viewed as part of the eternal cycle of reincarnation, there is no clear concept of "historical progress" in Buddhism.

Among the ancient peoples, the Chinese were far more historical in their thinking. But here too, we find the concept of a spontaneous, impersonal cosmic potential working throughout nature and human society. In spite of many exciting events recorded in history, Chinese historical thought was based upon the cyclic process of the universe. The basic causal factors moving human history were not of human volition, nor the will of a god, but the impersonal cosmic process that brought forth a myriad of changes without any direction.

The old Chinese classic, *I-Ching (The Book of Change)*, for instance, was entirely devoted to the question of change in the human world. Nature was conceived to be in a constant flux, *panta rhei* (everything flows); but going one step further, *I-Ching* describes the basic cause of change, be it natural or human, in terms of internality, not of externality. This is to say that all the phenomena of the world arise from the internal interaction of the two primary cosmic forces— the virile called the yang and the docile called the yin. Just as there are heaven and earth, male and female, long and short, and light and darkness, these two primary forces— which, despite their contradictory natures, are in fact complementary—produce all kinds of change. It is very interesting to note that the ancient Chinese concept of the basic building blocks of nature is similar to the plus-minus theory of modern electricity.

Later the Neo-Confucianism of the Sung Dynasty perfected Chinese cosmological thinking. Chou Tun-yi, for instance, held that before the cosmos as we now know it came into being and before the cosmic forces of yin and yang began to interact, there was something nebulous, silent, empty, unchanging, but self-sufficient. This *Rita*-like source of everything was called "the Great Ultimate." Chou explained that "the Great Ultimate through movement generates yang. When its activity reaches its limit, it becomes tranquil. Through tranquility the Great Ultimate generates yin. When tranquility reaches its limit, activity begins again. Thus movement and tranquility alternate and become the root of each other, giving rise to the distinction of yin and yang."[3] And then the interaction of yin and yang, as previously mentioned, produce the five basic elements of nature—water, fire, wood, metal, and soil. When these material forces (Ch'i) are distributed in harmonious order (Li), the myriad things of the universe, including human beings, are created.

Where did the Great Ultimate then come from? In dealing with this profound question, some Neo-Confucianists drew their thoughts from Taoism. They thought that "the Change as the Great Ultimate is fundamentally Ultimateless or Void, the Absolute Emptiness, which is without form."[4] This was the Non-Ultimate, which was, like Tao, an unnamable, eternal principle of nature. A formless form, thingless image, the Non-Ultimate was always nonexistent, but always existent, empty yet filled, blunted all sharpness but united all tangle. In brief, the ancient Chinese cosmology, like that of the Indians, did not have any clear concept of One Supreme God, the creator and the preserver of nature and human history.

In Chinese thought, the material and historical world was one inseparable continuum. Jung Young Lee, while discussing *I-Ching*, emphatically states that "we should look for spiritual processes similar to the physical processes," for "the 'I' is the microcosmic unit of all things, and the true self of each individual."[5] In so doing, Chinese thinkers regarded man as a part of nature, a microcosm, which reflected the organization of nature. About the human body, the *Huan-nan-tzu* said:

> Heaven has the four seasons, Five Elements, nine divisions, and three hundred and sixty days. Man likewise has four limbs, five viscera, nine orifices, and three hundred and sixty joints. Heaven has wind, rain, cold, heat, and man likewise has the qualities of accepting and giving, joy and anger. Therefore the gall corresponds to clouds, the lungs to vapor, the spleen to wind, the kidneys to rain, and the liver to thunder.[6]

Human life and society must be organized according to the principles of nature. Shih Huang Ti, for instance, built his palace on the model of nature, with as many rooms as the year had days. The palace decorations, too, had cosmic significance and symbolized the celestial lordship of the emperor. Likewise, a man's life must express the five basic moral principles—benevolence, righteousness, decorum, wisdom, and faith—on the basis of the five fundamental relationships: namely, loyalty between a king and a subject, filial piety between father and son, distinction between husband and wife, faith between friends, and order between the old and the young. In the end, the old Chinese philosophical schools almost invariably supported the status quo in lieu of historical change and progress. Confucius, for example, said: "If the price is not price, the minister not minister, the father not father, the son not son, then with all the grain in my possession shall I ever get to eat any?"[7]

In the West, especially in Greek philosophy, we trace the origin of speculations on the causal factors of historical change. Aristotle, for instance, thought a favorable climate was the primary causal factor for social and cultural development, and his climate hypothesis was later developed by Montesquieu in the eighteenth century. In our century, Ellsworth Huntington further elaborated upon this theory in his voluminous works such as *The Climatic Factor, Civilization and Climate*, and *Mainsprings of Civilization*. Carl Ritter of Germany and Henry Buckle of England in the nineteenth century advocated the theory of topography—a theory that the influence of land forms plays a vital role on the birth and growth of a civilization. In Asia, the popular belief in geomancy has similar ideas. On the other hand, Comte de Joseph Gobineau of France in the nineteenth century became famous by championing the idea that racial superiority of a nation is the most decisive factor in developing a civilization. His racism, so ardently expressed in his book, *The Moral and Intellectual Diversity* and *The Inequality of Human Races*, was echoed by Houston Chamberlain, an Englishman who married the daughter of Richard Wagner, in his book, *The Foundation of the Nineteenth Century*.

Among many historically untrained speculators Hegel, however, spurred the growth of metaphysical thinking on history more than anyone else. Borrowing the "dialectic" from ancient Greek philosophers such as Plato, Hegel framed the question of historical causation in terms of inevitable progress in the human world. Like others, he too saw contradictory phenomena so prevalent in time and in space in the world, and he pondered upon the interplay of opposing forces in making new chapters of history. As a philosopher, he discarded the prevalent hypotheses of monistic causes such as race, topography, climate, soil or natural resources; he also did not accept any of the multicausal theories of this time. Rather, like Shelling, Hegel conceived of the Absolute as the source of all diversity and multiplicity, "as a concrete Idea, as a concept unfolding by virtue of its own internal development."[8] To minds untrained in philosophy, this sounds very farfetched, and even unreasonable. But Hegel's Idealism was then a widely accepted philosophical scheme and he, in venturing into the realm of history, did not bother to reiterate his basic assumptions. If this was so, how could the Absolute unfold itself in the diverse phenomena of human affairs?

Here, he used dialectic extensively if not exclusively. Originally dialectic was an art of conversation used by Socrates. It involved the passing over of ideas into their opposites and the achievement of higher unity through inner contradictions and their synthesis. In Hegel's theory, dialectic is a "process in which a starting point is negated, thereby setting up a second position opposed to it and this second position is in turn negated, i.e., by negation of the negation, so as to reach a third position representing a synthesis of the two preceding, in which both are 'transcended,' i.e., abolished and at the same time preserved on a higher level of being." This third phase then becomes a new starting point of a new dialectic process.

By applying this dialectical method to human history, Hegel saw that the universal history of mankind is one grand dialectical progression, and in an upward spiral movement of time, treading through the long path of innumerable repetition of thesis, antithesis, and synthesis. But what made this triad of dialectical progression through historical time possible and so inevitable? Again his answer was simple. The historical movement of mankind was the self-revelation and self-realization of the Absolute Idea itself, and the Absolute was doing so not because of any external influence, but by its own inner necessity. The only essence of the cosmos was the Idea, and all other phenomena were means to be used for self-fulfillment.

The *Weltgeist* in Hegelian thought was none other than Reason, for the essential quality of spirit could not be described other than being reasonable. Since Reason revealed itself in human affairs as time went on, the world, as human history advanced, would therefore become a reasonable place to live. All the irrational elements pervasive in social institutions, economic systems, and political organizations would gradually be eradicated. In this sense, Hegel's philosophy of history was teleological.

Likewise, the fundamental attribute of the spirit, comparable to the gravity of matter, was freedom, not limitable by time and space, because man could not think of spirit as anything else other than being free. Therefore, the movement of history was equated with the progressive actualization of freedom from the stage of less freedom to the next stage of more freedom through the dialectical progress. Each historical epoch actualized this spiral-linear movement of freedom. At times, the course of events made human conditions appear very disorderly and confusing, but by virtue of the power of Reason which uses everything, including human passion—Hegel called it "the cunning of Reason"— the *Weltgeist* treads on, unveiling its inner structure and fulfilling itself in the course of time.

On the other hand, Karl Marx, using Hegel's dialectical method, contributed in his own way to the philosophy of history. Seeing the contradictory phenomena inherent in all human societies at all times, he also tried to discover some historical laws governing human progress. But contrary to Hegel's idealism, Marx based his thoughts on materialism, in the unswerving belief that "the world is by its very nature material." But the matter he conceived was not static as the Greek materialists previously thought. Rather, it was in constant motion, and consequently the world "develops in accordance with the laws of movement of matter."[9]

Contrary to Idealism, which upheld the supremacy of mind over matter, the Marxist materialist thought that "matter, Nature being, is an objective reality existing outside and independent of our mind; that matter is primary, since it is the source of sensations, ideas, mind, and that mind is secondary, derivative, since it is a reflection of matter, a reflection of being."[10] If matter is the essence and the cause of human history with its own ontological direction to move, what then put it into motion in the first place? Here, the question of the Prime Mover arises. But Marxism avoids the idea of believing in God as the Prime Mover by conceiving of matter as endowed with a mystical, or to a large extent deistic, power which sets its own law, the law of dialectical progress. The three major laws of matter in motion in the Marxist dialectical materialism, rearranged in a logical order, are as follows: 1) the law of the mutual interpenetration of opposites; 2) the law of the transformation of quantity into quality and vice versa; and 3) the law of the negation of the negation.

First, the law of the mutual interpenetration of opposites, although it was originally listed in second position, seems to me the true starting point of dialectical materialism. By conceiving of all motion as ultimately a "self-movement" derived from the "internal contradictions" of matter, it denies the existence of God. The impetus for change comes from the inner contradiction of matter, and from no other sources. A Soviet account of dialectical materialism published before 1938 states: "Contrary to metaphysics, dialectics holds that internal contradictions are inherent in all things and phenomena of Nature, for they all have their negative and positive sides, a past and a future, something dying away and something developing; and that the struggle between these opposites, the struggle between the old and the new constitutes internal content of the process of development."[11] Unlike the equilibrium theory of Comte and Spencer, Marxist dialectical materialism upholds the struggle of opposites as the basis of natural as well as social progress.

Second, the law of the transition from quantity to quality attempts to explain the cause of some metamorphic changes in human history. It assumes that once quantitative changes advance beyond "the limits set by the nature of the thing in question, a sudden shift from quantitative to qualitative change occurs; the thing ceases to be what it is and becomes something else." At this point, however, many illustrations provided by Soviet philosophers in an attempt to prove this axiom are unconvincing—for example, this illustration from an example in chemistry, saying the fact that "the various proportions in which oxygen combines with nitrogen or sulphur, each of which produces a substance qualitatively different from any of the other, is presented as a proof of this theory. In human society, the example of how a master-craftsman becomes a capitalist as soon as he accumulates a certain amount of money also illustrates this hypothetical law."[12]

Third, the law of the negation of the negation is even more mystical, or at least, it can hardly be understood by non-Communist intellectuals. The sudden change to a new quality does not remain in a static fixed form, but a new motion sets in dialectically as the new quality also becomes in turn the starting point of another movement when it is challenged by a new negation. Thus, the total movement of dialectical process continues on and on endlessly. In so doing, the past is not entirely liquidated, but rather sublimated into a new being. On this aspect, Lenin said that "it is not flat negation, nor casual, thoughtless negation, nor yet the wavering, doubting negation, that is characteristic and essential in dialectic. . .but negation as a moment of conjunction, as movement of development, in which the positive is conserved."[13]

On the basis of these speculative theorems of dialectical materialism, historical materialism sees the course of human progress in terms of a few qualitatively epoch-making stages of historical change; namely, from the primitive to the slave-owning society and feudal society, and thence to capitalistic society—all in the manner of the negation of the negation caused by the change of productive power entailing the change of productive relations. For instance, in the primitive society of communal land-ownership, the productive relations were based on the productive forces of primitive tools, skills, and techniques; but the introduction of the division of labor after the use of iron changed the whole social structure, transforming it into a new slave-owning society, and so forth.

The slave system broke down because of its inherent internal contradiction. It was unproductive and wasteful and had to be replaced by a feudal society, which in turn, because of its inner contradiction with the rise of the bourgeoisie, was replaced by capitalism. In this manner, Marxism forebodes the impending fall of capitalism mainly because of its internal contradiction developed by the ever-growing size of the proletariat. As more and more industrial plants are constructed, the capitalists are unwittingly digging their own grave.

Unlike changes in nature, the negation of the negation in human history can take place, according to historical materialism, by the conscious action of man too. The oppressed rise against the ruling class because of economic exploitation, and because the "surplus value" of labor is being taken away. Here the class struggle sets in. However, human will does not have its own autonomous rules but is rather the product of material conditions. In the *Communist Manifesto*, Marx and Engels stated clearly this cardinal point, saying, "Does it require deep intuition to comprehend that man's ideas, views and conceptions, in one word, man's consciousness changes with every change in the condition of his material existence in his social relations, and in his social life?"[14]

In reviewing these two schools of historical thought, Hegel's idealism and Marx's dialectical materialism, which in fact have become the two most influential philosophies of history in our age, my serious reservations about both lie in the fact that neither of them provides man with a proper place in history. If history is the progressive self-fulfillment of the Absolute Reason as Hegel claims, man becomes alienated from the mainstream of the historical world, reducing himself at best to a tool of the "cunning of Reason." By the same token, if dialectical materialism's claim that the law of matter in motion sets the course of human history, man's existence becomes meaningless. Man, in this case, being essentially matter, has no independent thought, except the capability of merely reflecting the existing material conditions in which he lives. Later Marx tried to recognize the will and energies, especially the collective will and energies of man by advocating the usefulness, if not necessity, of political revolution, but this ambiguity made his whole dialectical materialism fall into self-contradiction.

Even during the nineteenth century when Hegel and Marx attempted to reduce the complex causal factors of history into one single monistic law, there were many thinkers who refused to believe in the possibility of such reducibility. On the contrary, many of them viewed history as the product of multifarious human volitions. In the main, the thinkers who stood against one single system of history upheld the importance of heroes in the shaping of human destiny. Thomas Carlyle, for instance, wrote: "For, as I take it, Universal History, the history of what man has accomplished in the world is at bottom the history of the great men who have worked here. They were the leaders of men, these great ones, the modelers, patterns, and in a wide sense, creators of whatsoever the general masses of men tried to do or to attain."[15] Minos was regarded as the sole creator of the civilization of Crete, while Lycurgus was described as the constructor of Sparta. In the same vein, Asian historians attributed the creation of the Mongol Empire to the great leadership of Genghis Khan. In *The Will to Power*,

Friedrich Nietzsche wrote on the nature and quality of a hero who makes history:

> A great man—a man whom Nature has built up and invented in a grand style—What is such a man? First, he possesses the capacity of extending his will over great stretches of his life, and of despising and rejecting all small things, whatever most beautiful and "divine" things of the world there may be among them. Secondly, he is colder, harder, less cautious and more free from the fear of "public opinion";. . . Thirdly, he asks for no "compassionate" heart, but servants, instruments. . . He would rather lie than tell the truth, because lying requires more spirit and will.[16]

Sidney Hook tries to narrow the usual loose concept of greatness by distinguishing two kinds of leaders, "the eventful man and the event-making man." In his definition, the eventful man in history is "any man whose actions influenced subsequent developments along a quite different course than would have been followed if these actions had not been taken." Constantine, Washington, Jefferson, and a host of leaders belonged to this category. On the other hand, the event-making man "finds a fork in the historical road, but he also helps, so to speak, to create it." Caesar, Cromwell, and Napoleon belonged to this second category.[17] However, Leo Tolstoy held a strong position that besides kings, ministers, and generals, historians must study "the common, infinitesimally small elements by which the masses are moved."[18]

On the whole, this school of thought upholds that man, unlike animals which act on instinct, is essentially a rational being endowed with freedom, a special being capable of creating his own history. Henry Sidgwick says, "It is impossible for me to think at such a moment that my volition is completely determined by my formed character and the motives acting upon it. I exercise free choice as to which of the motives acting on me shall prevail."[19] Is a man then really autonomous in opting for his option? Are men, big or small, truly free to make decisions?

Among philosophers of history, we find more determinists than those who believe in man's freedom. Was Madame Pompadour really free in advising Louis XV to help Maria Theresa or was she a product of the *ancien regime*, who was subject to the tradition of her own days? In other words, could she do the same had she been born in another country at another age? Was President Harry S. Truman free in finalizing his decision to drop the atom bomb on Hiroshima? Or was he acting merely on the basis of the demand of his times?

We know so well that a historic character, however able and great, is first the product of his times, and his power only the result of various social forces. If the will of every man were free, if every man could act as he pleased, all history would be a series of disconnected incidents. If I examine an act that I performed a moment ago, I might think that I was free to do so; but if I reflect upon the same act ten years later, I may discover that my decision had a host of influences, both external and internal. To move or not to move my hands makes me feel to be perfectly free, but the very desire that causes my hands to move or not to move comes from necessity. Every human action, therefore, presupposes antecedents. In this sense, even Bismarck admitted that he was not free when he stated the following remark before the North German Reichstag on April 16, 1869:

> My influence on the events I took advantage of is usually exaggerated; but it would never occur to anyone to demand that I should make history. . . We cannot make history; we must wait while it is being made. We will not make fruit ripen more quickly by subjecting it to the heat of a lamp; and if we pluck the fruit before it is ripe, we will only prevent its growth and spoil it.[20]

Probably, it may be more apt to say that important individuals are important precisely as signs and symbols of different historical times. Baron Holbach wrote in *The Illusion of Free Will* that "man is born without his own consent. His ideas come to him involuntarily. His habits are in the power of those who cause him to act them. He is unceasingly modified by causes, whether visible or concealed, over which he has no control." Clarence Darrow, the famous American jurist, echoed Baron Holbach by saying that "We are all helpless. This weary old world goes on, begetting, with birth and with living and with death; and all of it is blind from the beginning to the end. Nature is strong and she is pitiless. She works in her own mysterious way, and we are her victims."[21] Mark Twain also held a similar view on the helplessness of man when he wrote: "Man is as purely a piece of automatic mechanism as is a watch, and can no more dictate or influence his actions than can the watch. He is flung head over heels into this world without even a chance to decline."[22]

There is the third school which, while regarding both freedom and determinism true, has tried to reconcile them. The major postulation of this school is that if we mean "free" to be entirely "uncaused," no man has ever been free; but on the other hand, if we mean free to be a man's capability to choose his action without being coerced, everybody is free. For example, when a man gives money to a beggar in deep sympathy, he is free in the sense that his decision is not coerced; but it holds equally true that his action, caused by human nature, is predictable inasmuch as most, if not all, human beings share the same sympathy in their hearts. A man can do what he wills to do, but he cannot be entirely free in determining what he wills.[23]

Among meta-historical thinkers, Sorokin and Toynbee tried to balance determinism and freedom. In a magnificently grand-scaled historical vista, and with scintillating and perspicacious insights, these men grouped, categorized, and compared major civilizations, dead and alive, and drew the conclusion that the natural world and human world are morphologically the same, with the similar, if not exactly identical, biological laws of life operating in both. Every civilization, just like a living organism, follows the cycle of life in terms of birth, growth, maturity, decline, and death. The single causal factor of history is the inner necessity of this law of biological life which moves in time in a cyclical pattern. But on this overall deterministic framework, they tried to reconcile the role of human freedom with history.

Toynbee is much less dogmatic and even less deterministic. Like Auguste Comte, he elucidated the concept of "modifiable inevitability." This is to say that man, to Toynbee, is essentially a spiritual being in the sense that he is capable of choosing between options in his efforts to improve his life. In *A Study of History*, he elucidates this point saying, "man can prevent potentially adverse laws from hindering him and can constrain potentially favorable laws to help him in the execution of his plans."[24] However, in so doing, Toynbee seems to have committed an illogical blunder which makes his whole system of thought logically inconsistent. Carl Wittke, one of my former professors, tells of his personal experience of talking with Toynbee. When asked why he could not have gone logically all the way through in upholding his cyclic theory of historical change, Toynbee paused for a moment and then said that he had a few grandchildren. How could he tell his grandchildren that their future was doomed and that doomsday would fall upon them?

This episode demonstrates, to some extent, the impossibility of deducing, inferring, and drawing historical law from the available source materials. In his strong argument against all kinds of historical determinism—cyclic, linear, dialectical, and evolutionary—Karl Popper points out that in history "the facts at our disposal are often severely limited and cannot be repeated or implemented with a preconceived point of view." He even ventures to say that "there can be no history of the past as it actually did happen; there can only be historical interpretations, and none of them final; and every generation has a right to frame its own."[25] A similar sentiment is echoed in Allan Bullock's *The Historian's Purpose:* "The historian does not believe that you can annex history to a metaphysical system or turn it into a science on that out-of-date nineteenth century model on which the original expectations of social sciences were founded."[26]

Instead of getting ourselves involved in an endless polemic, it may be perhaps more rewarding for us to proceed from a point which all the aforementioned historical theories seem to agree upon. Regardless of what position he takes, every philosopher agrees that history is the story of man. God does not need a history of His own because he is omnipotent. Nature has a natural history of the world, but in a strict sense it is not a real history, for natural changes are predetermined by natural laws. Conversely, if a man is entirely omitted from historical writing, the writing may become meaningless.

In short, historical questions can be boiled down to one deeper, more fundamental question, "What is man?" Undeniably, a man is a product of his environment, but he can, in a limited way, remold his milieu. The result of this dialectical tension between existing socio-cultural conditions and man's volition creates history. But how? As Martin Heidegger so sagaciously points out, human reality cannot be defined because "it is not something given, it is in question." A man is a possibility with unlimited power to be, and his life is becoming, ever becoming in time and in space.[27]

2. RELIGION AS A PROGRESSIVE-DETRIMENTAL FACTOR

From ancient times, philosophers in the East as well as in the West have attempted to answer the question, "What is man?" Even today this question is left largely unanswered.

The many divergent views of man represent an ever-widening spectrum of thought that merely confuses us. Some have thought that a human being is simply his body and nothing else. Friedrich Nietzsche, for one, said, "Body am I entirely, and nothing more, and soul is only the name of something in the body." On the other hand, some have thought that a man is something more than his body, something over and above his physical existence which can be called spirit—a quality that cannot be limited by space and time.[28] Thomas Carlyle said: "Man has a soul as certainly as he has a body; nay, much more certainly; properly it is the course of his unseen spiritual life, which informs and rules his external visible life."[29] He was more sure of his mental existence than his physical existence.

In a way, our efforts to study the question "What is man?" resemble the Chinese story of three blind men trying to find out what an elephant is like. The first blind man, after examining the elephant's legs, says that the elephant must look like columns; the second, after passing his hands over the elephant's belly, insists that it must look like a wall; and finally, the third, after touching its tail, asserts that the elephant must look like a snake. Every one has partial truth, but none the whole truth. Like the blind men, we see man from different angles and then talk in terms of one-sided definitions of this complex existence.

Man is *homo faber, homo sapiens, homo ludens,* and *homo esperans* according to which angle you are looking at him from. Man is a social animal, as Aristotle said; he is an animal that bargains, as Adam Smith said; he is an imitative creature, as Johann Schiller said; he is a power-craving animal, as Friedrich Nietzsche said; and he is a sexual animal, as Sigmund Freud said. Man is all of these, and much more. He is good as well as bad; he is rational as well as irrational; he is incredibly wise as well as unbelievably stupid. He loves and hates, hopes and despairs, and creates and destroys throughout his life.

Unlike the study of other objects which exist outside of

us, the identity of man is a question about ourselves; and therefore, regardless of how hard we may try to be objective, subjective elements creep into our thoughts, blinding our views and confusing us. Despite the tremendous knowledge we possess, we still have not enough knowledge about man himself. Historians do not know enough about the course of events since man first emerged on earth; anthropologists do not know enough about the characteristics, customs, habits, and evolution of man; physiologists do not know enough about the physical organism of man; and psychologists do not have enough knowledge about man's psychic world. Because of our inability to transcend ourselves, we cannot see the total picture of man objectively.

Suffice it to say that man cannot discover his nature in the same way that he detects the nature of physical properties. Man is different from animals for a variety of reasons. Compared to animals, man is physically ill-equipped to react to external stimuli. He cannot react to a physical danger as swiftly as a tiger. He is not as nimble, agile, and alert as a cat. When food is offered, an animal snatches it right away as its instinct dictates; but man has to decide whether it is proper for him to take it. He is a thinking animal. And much more than that, he thinks practically, rationally, emotionally, as well as symbolically. Ernst Cassirer points out that "Between the reactor system and the effector system which are to be found in all animal species, we find in man a third link which can be described as the symbolic system." Man lives not only in the physical universe but also in a symbolic universe, and his language, myth, art and religion are parts of his symbolic universe.[30]

The early Greeks also recognized the basic difference between man and animals. Plato and other Greek philosophers held that man is a dual being which has both body and mind. Man is a physical being constituted of matter. As a physical being, he has to eat and consume material goods, and in so doing, he must satisfy a number of desires. But certainly he is more than a mere physical body, for he feels, thinks, hopes, fears, expects, and chooses. God has no physical body and an animal has no mind; man alone has both body and mind.

Reasonable as it sounds, however, the concept of the duality of man cannot answer all the questions, and on the contrary, many more serious questions arise because of it. What is mind? Does it have any material substance? Is it made of many components such as reason, emotion, intuition, and will? If so, how do these various components work within the mind harmoniously? These are the questions that both philosophers and psychologists have tackled for so long without reaching any common consensus.

How does mind communicate with body? The Greeks, as in the case of Plato, believed in the duality of mind and body without similarity or direct relation between them. They thought that "the body is the prison-house of the soul." Descartes also thought that both are different substances, utterly different in basic natures. Kant thought mind is a spiritual substance, indestructible and immortal, while body is finite and destructible. On the other hand, sceptics such as David Hume proposed the bundle theory which says that the mind is nothing more than the collection of different perceptions. William James attempted to sweep away the questions on mind, saying that mind is the stream of consciousness.

Even today, notwithstanding the phenomenal growth of human knowledge, the precise relationship between the mind and the body remains undetermined. There are many complicated theories, such as epiphenomenalism, parallelism, and agnostic interactionalism. But instead of delving into these conflicting views, I would rather present my own concept of man.

I believe that man is a totality, not a duality, of spirit and body. Some Christian theologians have held the tripartite nature of man; namely, the theory that man is a complex of body, soul, and spirit. Irenaeus, for instance maintained: "One of these saves and fashions—that is, the spirit. Another is united and formed—that is, the flesh; while that which lies between the two is the soul, which sometimes follows the spirit and is raised by it, but at other times sympathizes with the flesh and is drawn by it into earthly passions." Erasmus also said, "The spirit makes us gods, the flesh makes us beasts, the soul makes us men."[31] Of course, as previously mentioned, man can be described in more variegated terms such as soma (body), psyche (soul), sarx (flesh), or pneuma (spirit) depending on the point of view from which he is being considered. But I believe that man is a psychophysical unity—a flesh-animated-by-soul as J. A. T. Robinson describes—rather than a tripartite being.

The Old Testament seems to make no dissection of man. Rather we find man as a unity of personality. Genesis 2:7 says: "And the Lord God formed man of the dust of the ground, and breathed into his nostrils the breath of life; and man became a living soul." This portion of the Scriptures makes clear that man, although partially matter and partially spirit, is a creative synthesis of both matter and spirit. He is a living soul.

More often than not, we are confused by various terms describing the immaterial part of a human being, the terms such as soul, spirit, mind, reason, and sense. To me, however, each word, with its own unique etymological history, describes the same thing, namely the nonphysical aspect of man. The term "mind", for instance, means the intellectual capacity of man to think, "reason" the ability of man to think logically, and both "spirit" and "soul" the godlike quality of man. To subdivide man's qualities and characteristics into the many categories that these terms connote would be unproductive and meaningless, for man as a total personality cannot be so dissected. Genesis 1:27 says, "So God created man in his own image, in the image of God created he him."

The very fact that a man talks of himself in terms of "I" stems from the reality that he is a spiritual being in bodily form. A man's thoughts grow in their constant relation to external stimuli, but at the same time they keep on going also without outside stimulation. This is a very important point to remember when evaluating man's role in history. If a man acts solely on the basis of his interaction to external circumstances like the feedback system of a computer, he cannot be a free agent in the creation of history; but since his essence, an image of God, does not depend upon external circumstances, he takes actions in accordance with the inner attitude of his spirit.

History comes to have meaning only when man is regarded as a being in God's image, an *embodied spirit*.[32] Animals cannot create history, for they act on instinct without reflective thoughts either before or after taking action. Only man, as an *embodied spirit*, can steer the course of his life. He is constantly making choices among possible alternatives, taking moral responsibility for his actions. But as a created being man cannot be the master of his own destiny. By God's grace, he can be a partaker in the creation of history.

What we call reason is a part of this unique quality of man as an *embodied spirit*, a special gift of God which enables him to think things out logically. But reason alone cannot spur a man to act. It must be balanced and harmonized with another quality of man—human will, which also is a special gift of God. A man with these qualities can make decisions or choices in steering his course of life; but moreover, as a physical being, he expresses his thought through the use of matter. No thought can be viable, creatively expressive, without using material forms. Thus, through man's thought and action, both pure thought and pure matter can really interact meaningfully—the results of their continuous interactions in time-spatial dimension becoming human history. Albert Dondyene, a Belgian philosopher, writes:

> In the objective sense, civilization and culture refer to the totality or objective products by means of which man re-

creates his surroundings and makes them serve the purpose of his life and spirit. Thus he transforms them into a human milieu, into what we have called "a world," a world of culture which is man's creation, a product in which he expresses himself and in which he is mirrored. In this sense, language and writing, works of art and monuments, literature and scientific works, social and political institutions, laws and administration of justice are "objects of culture." Hegel called them the world of the objective spirit, that is, of the spirit which expresses itself, objectivates itself in objects.[33]

At the same time, however, man is a social being. His action is societal. If left completely alone with no contact with other fellow human beings, a man may become either crazy or else degenerate into a brutish being. Only in group life does a man discover his individuality, with his unique talents and weaknesses. For instance, a man and a woman cannot fulfill their physical potentialities until they marry and raise their children. In social life man externalizes his potentialities and perfects his personality. This very capacity of fulfilling himself in social life lies in man's uniqueness as a historical being. History is, after all, the story of men in their social life.

Society does not have a life of its own in the same manner that a biological organism has. Nor does it have the spirit, soul, mind, reason, intellect, and will comparable to what an individual possess. But by the same token, society is not a mere aggregation of the atomized individuals who constitute it. Society has a milieu, the product of its own physical and spiritual environment in history-time, and this milieu has a long life-cycle, much longer than a human being. In today's terminology, society is a gigantic system composed of a myriad of subsystems such as political organizations, economic systems, class cleavages, and religious and cultural associations. This system in historical time is known as civilization, and in Toynbee's schematic classification there have existed twenty-one species of civilization in world history, each having a unique life-cycle.

Now then, what is the mainspring of life-force which has given life to these civilizations? What are the major factors which have enabled each civilization to grow or to decline? As previously pointed out, many theories have thus far attempted to pinpoint one single factor, as in the case of Marx's economic determinism, Gobineau's racial determinism, and Buckle's topographical determinism. Today many thinkers try to avoid the pitfalls of determinism by adhering to ambivalent multicausal hypotheses.

Nevertheless, if we are to accept the idea that man is an *embodied spirit* and history is the externalization of his potentialities, civilization can likewise be viewed as the *exteriorization* of the collective mind of the people in that society. This is to say that in social life, human beings develop a spiritual environment which influences individual minds and can be affected by the great ideas of the resolute-will-power of heroic individuals. Thrown into an already existing spiritual milieu at the time of his birth, a man may rebel, resist, assail the collective mind of his society, or even get away from it by migrating into other countries. But usually he absorbs, improves, and develops the spiritual milieu in which he lives.

In history we see the original emergence of collective mind in familism and tribalism. Even today, each family, according to its own unique historical traditions and social background, maintains a spiritual milieu which exerts decisive influence upon the formation of the children's personality. Each ethnic group may or may not develop a certain collective mind which conditions individual thought-patterns. What we call nationalism is a large form of collective mind. When the world shrinks in the space-time dimension as rapidly as it is now, all the peoples of the world may nurture a grand mankind-consciousness or a universal spiritual *milieu*.

I believe that this spiritual milieu constitutes the substructure of a society or a civilization on which political, social, economic, artistic, and other superstructures are built. My position on this fundamental question runs directly counter to Marxism. If the collective mind changes because of some internal or external factors, the whole civilization changes accordingly. At this point, however, I disagree with Hegel's theory of *Weltgeist*. Whereas Hegel held that the *Weltgeist* or the objectified world spirit progresses to fulfill itself by dint of its own innate laws, I assert that the collective mind of a civilization cannot exist by itself apart from individual minds; nor can it express itself without human actions. It exists in the majority of people in a society, but a determined minority or even an individual can change or reshape it.

When a spiritual milieu becomes incapable of coping with changing historical conditions often a small minority, with a new dynamic spirit, may effect historical changes by changing the spiritual milieu. We see historical cases proving this fact in the rise of Christianity in the Roman Empire, and the rise of Bolshevism in the Tzarist Russia. In both cases, history was changed not by nonhuman conditions such as climatic or topographical cataclysms, but by the conscious actions of determined human wills. Therefore, a jump into a new transfiguration of history or *Auheben* can be possible only when some people are united spiritually to achieve a certain common goal.

A new question arises here. What then generates, vitalizes, and perpetuates the spiritual milieu of a society? Marxism has a ready-made answer which holds that the human spirit cannot be anything more than the reflection of a given economic condition. To simplistic minds this sounds plausible. Our minds, individual and collective, are affected by environmental influences. The changing weather exerts its influence upon our feelings. The sunny climate of the Mediterranean makes the Italian national character merry and cheerful, but the dreary and cold weather of the Baltic region makes the Scandinavian people gloomy and austere. The value standards of the "haves" and the "have-nots" in every society are quite different. But these are rather sweeping generalizations. Not all Italians are happy-go-lucky; nor are all Scandinavians gloomy in temperament. The Gracci brothers of Rome and the Kennedy brothers of the United States were all reform-minded in spite of their wealth.

Therefore, no one can impugn the salient fact that our minds can think with or without external stimuli. Our minds can meditate, contemplate, and reflect on things that we never saw or heard. Abstract concepts like justice, freedom, and humanity exist in our minds, even though we have never seen them. We have no way to describe them in material forms. We believe in God, the most holy being who transcends time and space. In other words, man's mind is more than a mere conditioned response to material environment. It does react to external stimulus, but at the same time it can think autonomously.

Here, let us return to my belief that history is the externalized form of man's thought, individually and collectively. If a man is to *exteriorize* his thought, he must use material objects as tools. If a boy really loves his girl friend, one way to express his love is to give material gifts to her. Therefore, matter is not an independent entity with a value of its own; on the contrary man alone, while using matter to express his inner thoughts, creates new values. On the premise that "man perfects himself only by perfecting the universe," Albert Dondeyene observes:

> It is impossible to accomplish even our "immaterial" aspirations without the assistance of matter. No science is possible without laboratories; no aesthetic sentiment has any value as long as it is not expressed in a work of art; there is no poetry without language; no philosophical life without books of philosophy; no social life worthy of man without social institutions and positive laws; no lofty moral life without good conduct, for good intentions alone do not suffice to turn us into good men.
> There can be no culture in the subjective sense, that is, no

self-realization of the human subject, without the ensemble of objective creations by which nature is transformed into a world of culture.[34]

If we are to accept Thomas Carlyle's dictum that "mind is the creator and shaper of matter," what then constitutes the mainspring of the collective mind or the spiritual milieu of a civilization? Moral teaching, aesthetic education, and philosophical training all share their influences upon the formation of a spiritual milieu, but no one can deny the paramount influence of religion on the gestation and growth of "a complex set of interlocking beliefs which may be called a world-view."[35]

Moral doctrines are useful for educating man to be good, but they cannot change him completely. Philosophical teachings can be good for enlightening man, but they cannot completely remold him. Kant was great. So was Hegel. But how many of us can understand them? How many of us today want to follow their teachings? In this sense, it goes without saying that religion has been the most powerful spiritual force in directing human beings and shaping human destiny. Religion has been the basic psychosomatic matrix of individuals and cultures. It has expressed itself in political structures, economic systems, social stratification, and cultural traits. In *The Religious Experience of Mankind*, Ninian Smart writes:

> Throughout history and beyond in the dark recesses of men's earliest cultures, religion has been a vital and pervasive feature of human life. To understand human history and human life, it is necessary to understand religion.
> But religion is not something that one can see. It is true that there are temples, ceremonies, and religious art. These can be seen, but their significance needs to be approached through the inner life of those who use these externals.[36]

There have of course been many other factors which influenced the growth of cultures. In this scientific age religion no longer enjoys the power it wielded in the past. Many Western societies are fast becoming areligious. Yet as long as man, being mortal, remains ignorant of where he came from and where he is going he cannot be completely areligious. Even in atheistic societies like the Soviet Union, Marxism has become a "secular gospel" with elaborate symbols and rituals to satisfy the religious needs of the people. In the United States, which has long been dominated by materialism, we see the resurgence of religion today. Many Asian religions have been widely accepted by American youth. In the rapidly secularized Asian societies, on the other hand, nationalism often assumes the role of religion with semi-deified national heroes. Therefore, contrary to what Karl Marx expected, religion is not the opium of the people and it will not disappear from the earth, no matter how great the strides of science.

As Pitrim Sorokin maintains, "Each of the vast cultural systems is based upon some major premise, which the civilization articulates in the process of its life-career," and the "premise" that each civilization has is religion. "If religion is a matter of ultimate concern, and society is a common system of ultimate-value attitudes," writes John M. Magee, "then it follows that Tillich's view of religion as the substance of culture and culture as the form of religion makes good sense."[37]

I believe, therefore, that the twenty-one civilizations that Arnold Toynbee so elaborately classified were all born of religions. One religion or a group of religions (as in the case of China) formed the psychosomatic matrix of a society and expressed beliefs and principles in the myriad facets of the civilizations. The different national ethos of each people evolved from a set of interlocking beliefs which we broadly call religion. Where then did religions come from?

No one explanation for the origin of the various religions is tenable. Psychologists such as C. G. Jung, sociologists such as Emile Durkheim, and philosophers such as John Dewey have provided us with divergent views on the origin of religions. As a Christian, however, I believe that man, being created in God's image, cannot rest until he finds Him. Undoubtedly man's fear of natural forces caused him to believe in something supernatural. Inasmuch as God has revealed Himself in nature and in history, man can find at least some of His attributes there. Yet, being limited in understanding, man's efforts to find supernatural power often results in superstition. Unless we come to believe in what God revealed of Himself in Jesus Christ we cannot know God as He is.

At any rate, without a proper understanding of the great religious traditions of the East, we have no way to appreciate the Asia of the past, nor can we properly observe the present transitional characteristics of our age. Hinduism, Buddhism, Confucianism, Taoism, and to a lesser extent, Shamanism and Shintoism all had their share in giving birth to, and in promoting, the cultural progress of Asian societies. Under the tidal challenge of the modern "secular gospels" such as liberal democracy, socialism, Communism, and nationalism, the psychic forces of these traditional religions are currently lying beneath the surface as though they may soon disappear entirely. But they are still here under the deep substrata of the Asian psyche.

Viewed broadly with a cross-cultural comparative perspective, Hinduism, Buddhism, Confucianism, Taoism, Shamanism, and Shintoism were, in spite of the obvious differences among them, the same in that all of them were basically naturecentric. None of them had a clear concept of one personal God, the Creator and the Preserver of the universe and human society.

In brief, these naturecentric religions shaped the spiritual milieu of the Asian civilizations. Religions were the mainspring of ancient music. Songs praised nature deities and dances were aimed at repelling evil spirits. Sculpture created idols, the images of gods, and architecture was developed with the construction of temples and shrines. Kings played the dual roles of priest and administrator.

These religions created human societies by teaching people virtues such as loyalty, justice, filial piety, tolerance, humanity, sincerity, and purity—all based upon the concept of natural law governing the universe and human society alike.

However, as time went by, these religions, becoming hardened in institutional structures, also exerted detrimental and adverse effects upon Asian civilizations. By deifying natural forces and worshiping them, people could not exercise their freedom to make social progress. In his "I-Thou" relationship with nature, the Asian could not "subdue" the earth for his benefit. However hard a man might try to free himself from the bondage of nature, he still was a captive, fatalistic, and impotent being.

History became eventless in spite of many events recorded in its annals. It was regarded as the cyclic, meaningless movement of time. Since historical time progressed in cyclic forms, leading nowhere, the innumerable dynastic changes, wars, rebellions, and intellectual innovations had no intrinsic value other than that of edifying human minds. The basic sociopolitical structure of each civilization remained the same. In other words, the ancient Asian religions, despite their great contributions to the birth and growth of the respective civilizations, eventually came to show marginal utility. To be sure, without their spiritual support, the ancient Oriental civilizations could not have been sustained; but in so doing, the law of antinomy became evident: these religions, while sustaining the civilizations, became at the same time stumbling blocks to social progress.

3. BIBLICAL FORMULA FOR HISTORICAL PROGRESS

In this respect, the appearance of the Old Testament marked a Copernican turning point in human history. Only Judaism refused to be naturecentric. It did not revere, venerate, and worship nature. Instead of deifying natural forces as did other religions, the Judaic religion challenged, de-mythologized and desacralized nature. In the Bible, nature had no mystical power by which it could control human destiny; it was "noneternal, created, dependent, and operating only through the power of a transcendent deity."[38] To put it differently, the desacralization of nature was only possible through faith in the omnipotent, om-nipresent, omniscient, and transcendent God as the Creator and the Preserver of all existing beings, material and spiritual. God was not in nature, nor a part of nature. He was beyond time and space.

How did the Jews produce such uniquely sublime religious ideas? Was it due to their usual religious genius or to the anomalous severity of the natural environment in which they lived? I should like to express my conviction that the Bible was a special revelation from God. The revelation of God's works in nature and in human history could be comprehended and appreciated by man's reason—another gift from God—but man's search for God with his thought alone fell far short of being sufficient to understand Him; but now God spoke to men through His revealed Words. No human speculative thought could arrive at such truths, so divinely pure and novel. Paul Tillich thus comments on the historical birth of the biblical religion:

> The command to Abraham to leave his homeland and his father's house means the command to leave the gods of soil and blood, of family, tribe and nation; that is, the gods of space, the gods of paganism and polytheism, the gods who stand beside each other—even if one of them is the most powerful.
>
> The true God who spoke to Abraham cannot be identified with a family or city-God.
>
> The threat which we hear first in the words of Amos is the turning point in the history of religion. It is unheard of in all other religions that the God of a nation is able to destroy His nation without being destroyed Himself. In all other religions the god dies with the people who adore him.[39]

The biblical doctrines of God, nature, and man were essentially for the spiritual life of man, and certainly not for the creation of any mundane civilization. Unlike today's secular ideologies, they did not provide people with a blueprint for any version of utopia. Nor were they interested in what kind of polity, economic system, social structure, and cultural life people should create. But contradictory as it may seem, in their very unworldly teachings lay the seeds of social progress as well as man's spiritual growth. This statement may sound paradoxical, but truth, like a precious jewel, is hidden from insensitive eyes. The biblical teachings such as "Love your enemy" or "To give is better than to receive" do not make any sense if viewed by reason alone, but they prove themselves to be self-evident in the lives of those who put them into practice. Likewise, we can say that even the most supernatural and spiritual instructions of the Bible produced many effects upon the historical progress of mankind.

Let us first take as an example the concept of God in the Bible and its effects upon human progress in history. Genesis 1:1 says that "In the beginning God created the heaven and the earth," thus depicting Yahweh as the Creator of the universe *ex nihilo*. Again, in Exodus 3:14, where Moses challenged God asking Him who He was, the reply was "I am that I am." God was not in nature; nor was He a personification of natural forces. He transcended the time and spatial dimension in which we live and think. The actual effect of this belief in the One Supreme God upon human civilization was tantamount to a spiritual revolution, for by putting his faith in God, man could liberate himself from the superstitious fear that he has in nature and pave the way for scientific and technological development. In place of the old naturecentric world views, a new theocentric *weltanshauung* came into being. Therefore, by believing in one personal God the Jews overcame the shortcomings of the many false world views based on *Rita, Tao,* or the Great Ultimate.

The concept of nature became clearer. Nature had no mystical power over man, for it was created by God. But the Bible did not tell Adam and Eve that they could conquer, plunder, and destroy nature at will. In Genesis 1:28 God said to them, "Be fruitful, and multiply, and replenish the earth, and subdue it; and have dominion. . .over every living thing that moveth upon the earth." In effect, Adam and Eve were told that they did not possess the Garden of Eden. Merely, it was entrusted to them so that they could maintain and manage it for the glory of God. Therefore, the biblical doctrine instructs us that we do not possess nature, nor the right to pollute and damage it for selfish reasons. Nor do we own any material property as our own. As God's stewards, we simply manage material goods to render glory to God. This concept of material possession later became a cardinal economic ethical foundation of modern capitalism.

According to these biblical doctrines, man's position in the universe became clear. No longer was he the child of nature who, chained by the law of necessity and psychologically intimidated by natural forces beyond his control, found no freedom of action in life. He was a created being, but unlike other created beings, he was created in the image of God (Genesis 1:27). Being so, man was a rational being endowed with the capacity of thinking. In the image of God lay the spirituality of man. Being rational and spiritual, man is a free agent, for as Hegel pointed out, whereas the essence of matter is gravity, that of spirit is freedom. However, in no sense does the Bible say that man's rationality and spirituality are unlimited.

In the biblical concept of man, the concept of sin as the explanation of man's basic condition is unique. Ancient Chinese philosophy did not recognize sin. Both good and evil were regarded as something essentially inherent to nature—a result of Heavenly principles. Confucianism, notably in the doctrines of Mencius, maintained that man was basically good and everybody could become a sage through learning and self-discipline. Man suffered because

of ignorance and not because of sinful nature. Among the
many ancient sacred books, only the Bible presented a
realistic view of man who, through his false pride and desire to become like gods, committed sin and fell from the
grace of God. Therefore, by recognizing their own sinful
nature, the Jews could prevent themselves from falling into
the pitfall of anthropocentrism.

But even as a sinner, man is still loved by God or, better,
the grace of God has perpetuated history in spite of human
iniquities. Both Adam and Eve were allowed to "till the
ground" for their living and for the creation of culture
(Genesis 3:23). Even Cain, after murdering his own brother
Abel, was protected by God's love. Sinner that he was,
"Cain builded a city, and called the name of the city, after
the name of his son, Enoch" (Genesis 4:17). Thus, the biblical doctrine of man obviates the "romantic error of seeking
for the good in man-as-nature and for evil in man-as-spirit
or reason, and also obviated the idealist error of regarding
man's mind as good or body as evil."[40] In thought and
action man must be aware of his potential as being created
in God's image and his limitations as a being with a sinful
nature. Only in God's grace can he be really creative.

Suddenly history came to have meaning. God became the
God of history, not merely of the world after death, for He
revealed Himself in historical time and fulfilled His will in
history. History was no longer an endless cycle going on
eternally and leading nowhere. Life on earth was not an
illusion but had positive meaning. In God's eternal plan,
human history had its origin, process, and goal—the alpha
and the omega. God acted in historical time toward a final
goal. Also, for the first time in human history, the Bible
described man's record as a universal history, negating national boundaries. In Abraham all nations were blessed, not
merely the Jews alone. The whole universal history of mankind was viewed as a linear progression fulfilling God's
final goal. Yet instead of being a prosaic, placid linear
progression on a predestined scheme, history was interwo-

ven with the continuous dialectical tension between the downward movement of man's sinful nature and the upward movement of God's grace. Constantly and persistently, God called his prophets and gave them missions to perform; and men, by responding to God's call willingly, partook in the creation of new history. 1 Samuel 3:4, for instance, says, "The Lord called Samuel, and he answered, 'Here am I.' " In this calling and answering between God and man lies the profound interaction of the divine with human beings, the interaction which sustains and promotes history.

Today, in our secular age in which people imbued by worldly thoughts are prone to underrate the Jewish contributions to human progress, one may argue that the Hebrew people, despite their lofty religious ideals, failed to develop science, technology, arts, and democratic principles—the elements which have given birth to modernization. To a certain extent, this contention is true. The reason for this cultural unproductiveness in spite of the rich spiritual foundation is not, however, entirely inexplicable. Perhaps the fact that the Old Testament was not fully compiled until the end of the Babylonian Captivity in the fifth century B.C. partially explains the lack of time for the Jews to *exteriorize* the potent spiritual forces in their civilization. The Jews became so full of self-righteousness and self-complacency by taking pride in themselves as a chosen people that their national life veered from the biblical path.

In any case, my point is that the Hebrew civilization, even with its many weaknesses, laid the spiritual groundwork for the sociocultural progress of mankind. Without the biblical desacralization of nature, no true scientific inquiries could have been possible. Without the Torah's concept of placing law above man regardless of his social position, no spirit of democracy could have been grounded in human minds. Without the meaning of history being brought into line with biblical principles, no idea of historical progress could have germinated. My contention is

that we must give due credit to the invaluable contributions
that the Hebrew tradition made to humanity.

Against this historical background, Jesus came to earth at
the right time to redeem men, thereby fulfilling one historical period. But at the same time, by His resurrection, He
inaugurated a new historical period which in due course of
time will be fulfilled by his Second Coming.

It goes without saying that Jesus did not preach social
progress. He did not speak about economic development.
He did not show people any utopian blueprint. He spoke
only of the Gospel, the good news of man's salvation. How
could this most unworldly message generate, spur and pro-
pel social and economic progress in Western civilization?
The historical view of Jesus was eschatological, if not
apocalyptic; but paradoxically enough, in his very eschatological message lay the source of power which moved
the West progressively. Jesus constantly denounced the
things of the "world"—money, fame, material blessings,
power, etc.—but when people accepted his Gospel and
likewise denounced the "world" as Jesus taught them to do,
they, paradoxically, became materially successful as well as
spiritually blessed.

Therefore, the biblical formula for historical progress can
only be understood in paradoxical terms. It is not to be
equated with any sociopolitical ideologies or with any economic planning. Jesus was neither a political revolutionary,
nor a social reformer. Social and political reforms are always
necessary if we are to make historical progress, inasmuch as
our societies tend to fall into inequities. But the ideas of
reform based upon human planning, human reasoning,
and human visions have not lasted long. Without exception, reforms based on human reasoning have been ephemeral and evanescent.

On the contrary, the Bible, before touching upon problems within social institutions and political systems, directs
our attention to the most fundamental question—the question of the human heart, the mind of man which lies be-

neath all the superficial phenomena of history. By changing the innermost essence of man, the Bible exerts influence upon the whole direction of history. Historical progress is therefore a byproduct, rather than the basic goal, of the influence of the Gospel. When we accept the Gospel all sorts of worldly blessings shall be given to us as the byproducts of our new spiritual lives in Christ. This ~imple but cardinal truth was expressively revealed to us in the early ministry of Jesus. Matthew 4:12-17 describes the way that Jesus began his ministry on earth:

> Now when Jesus had heard that John was cast into prison, he departed into Galilee; and leaving Nazareth, he came and dwelt in Capernaum, which is upon the seacoast, in the borders of Zabulon and Nephthalim:
>
> That it might be fulfilled which was spoken by Esaias the prophet, saying, The land of Zabulon, and the land of Nephthalim, by the way of the sea, beyond Jordan, Galilee of the Gentiles;
>
> The people which sat in darkness saw great light; and to them which sat in the region and shadow of death light is sprung up.
>
> From that time Jesus began to preach, and to say, Repent: for the kingdom of heaven is at hand.

This passage depicts the dolorous, cadaverous condition of the people in Zabulon and Nephthalim on the shores of Galilee. Constantly battered by foreign hordes and eking out an indigent livelihood from the barren soils and the scanty supply of fish, they barely sustained their wretched life in the "darkness" and in the "shadow of death." To the people of Galilee, life was a continuous misery and history a meaningless cycle of despair. When Jesus, the Son of God, was ready to begin his ministry He decided to proclaim His Gospel to these ignorant people of Galilee instead of choosing the inhabitants of aristocratic Rome, cultural Athens, or commercial Alexandria.

To the people of Zabulon and Nephthalim who were

under the "shadow of death," Jesus did not proclaim any utopian blueprint, nor any sociopolitical ideology. His message had little to do with socioeconomic reforms or any revolutionary movement. On the contrary. the simple and straightforward message that Jesus preached was, "Repent: for the kingdom of heaven is at hand" (Matthew 4:17).

Realistically, he pointed out that man, blinded by his sinful nature, could not see the light of Truth. The cloud of darkness hovering over Zabulon and Nephthalim appeared not so much because of the irrationality in sociopolitical systems and organizations as because of man's sinful nature. Therefore, Christ told us that without tackling this fundamental question of sin—the alienation of man from God through the various forms of anthropocentrism—no individual or society can be wholesome. The awareness of sin and repentance in individual hearts is the spring of moral consciousness which can purify society and pave the road for historical progress.

Here again, the biblical way for historical progress can only be understood in paradoxical terms. History amply demonstrates that we can make historical progress in all realms of life only when individuals in repentance realize that social development "is not our primary but only our secondary task." In innumerable historical cases we find that "it was those Christian men and groups of men who did not believe in progress who did the most to move the world in real progress."[41] Penance can be the solid foundation of a sane civilization. Although the act of repenting itself must be done instantaneously, the process of repentance is, theoretically at least, divided into a few steps.

First, a man must recognize his sin as something very real and deadly in its consequences. This is a stage in which he becomes aware of his shortcomings, wrongdoings, and transgressions against God, against his fellowmen, and against himself. In doing so, he understands the simple but very important truth that he, as a being created, cannot be equal to the Creator. Only when a man comes to accept the fact of his being a sinner may he open his eyes to see the perverted relationship between God and him, nature and him, and his fellowmen and him. God's Kingdom is being created by the aggregation of sinners. It is paradoxically true that a society of "self-righteous" people becomes unavoidably dirty and corrupt, but a society of sinners, with its ever-renewing and ever-regenerating power, becomes much saner and cleaner.

Second, the act of repentance involves the stage of liberation, the liberation of man from his wrong world-views, beliefs, values, and norms which enslaved him in the past. Living in perpetual repentance is a work of continual liberation which makes a man truly free, not only from the sociopolitical establishment in which he lives, but also from his sinful nature. Here again we see a paradoxical truth in that a man of selfish freedom exists in a state of bondage, while a man of repentance can free himself from all the yokes of the world, even from the yoke of his own carnal self.

Third, the act of repentance can only be completed with the positive acceptance of Jesus as personal Savior. Christ—the Son of God—comes to live in a person's mind, guiding and directing his life like a new compass, the true spiritual compass. All the desires of man become sublimated, for from now on he, like Paul, eats, drinks, studies, plans, and works for the realization of God's will in his life.

In this sense, therefore, Christianity goes one step beyond individual repentance. In the second half of Matthew 4:17, Jesus made this fact clear by saying that "the kingdom of heaven is at hand," and then further clarified this statement in Matthew 6:33 by saying, "Seek ye first the kingdom of God, and his righteousness, and all these things shall be added unto you." Repentance is only the first step to enabling me to take part in God's providence in human history. Through accepting Christ in my heart, I should move forward instead of tarrying here. I can grow up in spiritual maturity by rendering myself to do the works which build the Kingdom of God. To me, from now on the highest value for which I should live and for which I must be ready to sacrifice all other values is the realization of His Kingdom. After hearing the voice of the Lord calling him to serve His Kingdom, Paul said that "what things were gain to me, those I counted loss for Christ" (Philippians 3:7). Making the Kingdom of God his highest priority, Paul pressed continuously, throughout his life, "toward the mark for the prize of the high calling of God in Christ Jesus" (Philippians 3:14).

To a man of God, history comes to have a new meaning, for he consciously partakes in the creative works of God. Of course, as long as he remains on earth, a Christian cannot get rid of the contradictory impulses of life—the paradoxes of love and anger, pity and severity, humor and sadness, simplicity and profundity, and obedience and rebellion—but while imitating the life of Christ, he too learns how to integrate these conflicting impulses into his new personality as a "new creature" in Christ.

In brief, Christianity is individualistic, but goes far above and beyond what individualism stands for. In place of individual pride, it demands penance; instead of seeking self-gains, it asks a man to be self-sacrificial. The Kingdom of God is likened to "treasure hid in a field." A man who finds this treasure will sell all possessions, material and intellectual, and buy the field (Matthew 13:44). It is like a specially valuable pearl. A merchant who knows its preciousness will sell everything he has, and will buy it (Matthew 13:45, 46). The Kingdom of God grows in a man's soul as he takes it as the highest goal and value of his life.

In this respect, I do not agree with the social Gospel which puts first priority on the salvation of society rather than of the individual. Superficially viewed, society looks like a living organism with its unique life-cycle and soul. Nowhere, however, does the Bible say that a society will stand before God in the last judgment; and, therefore, Christianity is at odds with collectivism, be it nationalistic or socialistic. What we call "the soul of a society" in line with Oswald Spengler's argument cannot be anything more than the spiritual milieu of a people, which has been produced over a long period of historical time.

And yet by the same token, we cannot deny that Christians while tarrying on earth must influence the biocultural milieu of the society in which they live. Man, being a social animal, cannot perfect himself except through contact with his fellowmen in society. Christ came to work for men and women, and by calling His disciples He worked for God's Kingdom collectively. Through a handful of followers who responded to His call in faith, Jesus ignited a new spiritual revolution which eventually conquered the mighty Roman Empire, tamed the Germanic barbarians, and influenced all mankind even until today.

Collectiveness is, therefore, an essential element in Christian enterprises, but in no way can it be identified as political or social collectivism. Christian collectiveness, with Christ as its head, stands far above and beyond any anthropocentric collectivism. Whereas secular collectivism lessens the sense of individual responsibility, Christian collectiveness makes individuals more mature spiritually.

Christians are for social reform, for social institutions have a profound influence upon the formation of individual personalities. A baby is born into a social milieu and forms his personality, by and large, under social influences that he cannot control. In this very aspect lies a popular misconception about Christianity. Many people historically untrained and intellectually unsophisticated think that Christianity is basically against reform and revolution. Their conservatism is misplaced, because what we have to conserve is not the present ecclesiastical hierarchy or any social establishment. Every man and every institution—be it religious or secular—is tainted with sin, and naturally both man and his social systems must change to improve themselves. Only self-complacency and pride can stop us from reforming ourselves. In this very fact of insisting on the importance of change lies the truth that Christianity is a revolutionary religion, undoubtedly the most revolutionary of the world's religions.

What we have to conserve is neither the present church structure nor its set of ritual practices, nor any social system in which the majority of people are Christians. On the contrary, the most important fact that we must conserve is the revolutionary tradition of Christianity which changes man, his family, his community, and ultimately his world. When a man accepts Christ as his Savior, he is turning not halfway from his previous sinful life; he must turn around completely. So must a society. By aiming at realizing the kingdom of God in the social milieu, a society must try to revolutionize itself constantly and perpetually. I believe that in this sense Christianity is not piecemeal reform, but perpetual revolution. Only for this reason, I am a conservative Christian; I am in favor of revolutionary changes in individual life and on a social plane so long as they are being brought forth by Christian means.

Christian beliefs revolutionize man and society in the use of freedom. A Christian, by virtue of having the seed of God's Kingdom growing in his spirit and liberating him constantly from the grip of sin, learns how truly to exercise his free will. In his grace, he can be prudent in using his freedom—the very God-given quality that Adam and Eve misused—so as not to be licentious or capricious. To surrender his will to God's service sounds like a sure way to be enslaved by a divine will, but the opposite is true. A man can become free, expanding the radius of his freedom, only when he surrenders himself to a higher law. This seemingly paradoxical truth is expounded by Arnold Toynbee:

Liberty from a lower law can never be purchased except at the cost of submitting to a higher law; and, when purchased at this cost, it can be preserved only at the price of eternal vigilance; for an empirically experienced hierarchical relationship between these diverse laws current in the Universe, which seems to certify that they are so many enactments of a single divine legislator, creates an agonizing conflict of law of God's creatures that have accepted His challenge to transfer their allegiance from some lower of His to some higher one.[42]

Next, Christian beliefs revolutionize man and society so they use reason as it ought to be used. Reason, too, is stained by sin, and therefore fallible. Without the grace of God it loses its power, and as a consequence all too often becomes a tool of evil. In Watergate, the culprits were not uneducated and unreasonable men. We see that inhumane crimes today are committed more by the white-collar workers than by the other groups. A highly rationalistic society without religious beliefs in God is as fragile and fallible as a house built on sand. In contrast, Christians knowing their limitations use their reason more carefully and conscientiously, lest they should become irrational in their efforts to be rational. Although the Kingdom of God can never be realized on earth, the spiritual force of these spiritual men can realize the image of the City of God in their respective societies.

Also, Christian beliefs revolutionize men and societies and make love a cardinal historical force. From time immemorial, many idealists have expressed the hope of creating a world of love, not of hatred and conflicts, only to find, to their dismay, their good will derided and their earnest efforts wasted. Only the transcendental grace of God coming from above enables us to love others. Only when we receive through faith the radiation of God's love—the perfect love—in our minds, can we love others. This love from beyond history is revealed to us in Jesus. The ultimate goal of our existence on earth is to realize the world of love as exemplified by Jesus on the cross.[43]

When then is the omega-point of human history? In sharp contrast to social ideologies which tell us that the final destination of history will be the perfection of democracy,

Communism, socialism, or anarchism, Jesus repeatedly and emphatically told us that "the kingdom of God is at hand." This passage makes it unequivocably clear that the omega-point of world history is not the perfection of the American model of democracy or the Soviet model of Communism, but the realization of God's Kingdom. We can keep making genuine historical progress only when we collectively set up our social goal of bringing forth His Kingdom on earth. This may sound very other-worldly, unpragmatic, and impracticable; but I believe that it is a dynamic teaching, both practical and real, for by setting their collective goal on establishing His Kingdom, the early Puritans in America, for instance, laid the foundation of what the United States has become today.

However, one caution at this point seems necessary. There is a fallacy prevalent among ultraconservative Christians who tried, quite awkwardly, to identify the Medieval West as the model for God's Kingdom, considering the two an inseparable unit called Christendom. This is far from being true. God's Kingdom is an eternal ideal, unrealizable and unattainable in historical time, and in this sense, neither the Medieval West nor the United States of the 1950s ever actualized it on earth.

The Kingdom of God, soaring above the time-spatial dimension of human life, must be the unchanging, eternal goal of every society—a goal which constantly spurs human progress. The Kingdom of God presently exists in the minds of true believers, but its perfection lies in the future. It is a perfect ideal society toward which human beings must perpetually move. By setting His Kingdom as our collective goal, we can always strive to reform, remodel, reshape, and regenerate our society, perfecting the shortcomings of sociopolitical ideologies.

In brief, the Kingdom of God is a divine milieu in which God's holy will dominates political institutions, economic systems, cultural traits, norms, and the behavioral patterns of people, in addition to man's innermost life. However the beneficiaries of such a milieu are men, not God, for "all things shall be added unto you" (Matthew 6:33). Let me explain this truth.

First, politically the Kingdom of God is the realm in which His righteousness rules over a people. How unbearable would it be if politics were dominated by man's trickery rather than God's justice? Second, economically the Kingdom of God is a milieu in which the people, recognizing God's sole ownership of all things existing on the earth, will act as His stewards and render their earthly possessions for the glory of God. Third, socially the Kingdom of God, although acknowledging the inequality of talents among people, seeks to establish freedom and equality among men and women on the basis of their inalienable rights as the children of God. Fourth, ethically the Kingdom of God is based upon love instead of servitude and bondage.

Therefore, to glorify God actually means to serve men. The Bible says that to give a glass of water to a child can be a tangible way to serve God. Theocentrism in this sense links directly to true humanism. In order to obey God, Christ gave His life for human beings, even to the point of death on the cross.

What we Asians living amid despair and chaos must do first is to stop searching senselessly for answers in secular ideologies. Such naiveté in the past has led us nowhere. Just as the Western models of liberal democracy and democratic socialism, and the Soviet model of Communism and Maoistic Communism, have been unproductive and even to some extent harmful and detrimental to our growth, so will the improvised, eclectic ideologies of Asia—Guided Democracy, True Democracy, New Democracy, and Nationalistic Democracy—undoubtedly become equally fruitless and even more woefully harmful. Man's reasoning power, stained by sin, cannot by itself discover the direction of historical change. Reason is a light, but without the grace of God, it is at best a dim light. Instead, we must seek his Kingdom as our new collective goal. Only such divinely inspired direction can 1) liberate us from our sinful natures; 2) revolutionize our minds and modes of life so that we may use properly the power of reason, freedom, and love; 3) keep our society from falling into self-righteous anthropocentrism or self-abnegating nihilism; and 4) enable us to partake in truly providential history-making.

Contradictory as it sounds, proclaiming the Kingdom of God, individually and socially, as our spiritual goal is dogmatic and liberal at the same time. It is dogmatic in the sense that it refuses to recognize any secular ideology as its equal, and liberal in the sense that it allows us to work out the detailed plans to implement its image on earth as best as we can. In other words, God's Kingdom transcends the time-space dimension of history, soaring high above any other ideas and ideals that man has developed, but still allowing us to exercise our freedom in thinking, planning, and working toward the goal. Herein lies the most exquisite beauty of the Kingdom of God as our spiritual goal: it is clear-cut in principle and ambiguous in implementation without self-contradiction.

Here is another seemingly self-contradictory fact of the Christian life. On one hand, the Christian faith is so unswervingly dogmatic that it forbids us to sway back and forth, but on the other hand it is so transcendental in doctrinal principles that it allows us ample room to use our freedom in the practical decisions in our daily life, so long as our moral compass directs us rightly toward God's Kingdom. It matters little whether Christians live in an agrarian society or in an industrial society so long as secular powers do not interfere with us unduly in our exercise of free will. But conversely, it matters seriously if political power impedes our freedom of choice.

Another striking aspect of the biblical doctrine of the Kingdom of God is its realism. Compared to the secular utopianism of Plato's *Republic* and More's *Utopia*, it is far more practical. Unlike secular ideologies, Christianity is not so naive as to believe that all the presently vexing social problems can be rectified by revolutions. By its insistence on concentrating on the problems of sin individually and institutionally, the Gospel brings forth fundamental changes in human history. Christ changes man, and by way of changing man, He regenerates society and provides civilization with a life-giving force.

The Bible is realistic, so realistic as to leave us no room to indulge in the naive hope that our efforts to evangelize Asia will automatically ameliorate the problems confronting us. The two cities—the City of God and the City of Man—will continue to exist in perpetual conflict until the very end of the world. In another parable of sowing, Jesus said:

> The kingdom of heaven is likened unto a man which sowed good seed in his field: But while men slept, his enemy came and sowed tares among the wheat, and went his way. But when the blade was sprung up, and brought forth fruit, then appeared the tares also.
>
> So the servants of the householder came and said unto him, Sir, didst not thou sow good seed in thy field? from whence then hath it tares? He said unto them, An enemy hath done this. The servants said unto him, Wilt thou then that we go and gather them up?
>
> But he said, Nay; lest while ye gather up the tares, ye root up also the wheat with them. Let both grow together until the harvest: and in the time of harvest I will say to the reapers, Gather ye together first the tares, and bind them in bundles to burn them: but gather the wheat into my barn (Matthew 13:24-30).

In historical time, the Kingdom of God grows slowly, for evil apparently grows more vigorously. As science progresses and technology advances, evil forces will become more and more sophisticated. But the Kingdom of God will continue to grow, not because of man's efforts, but by the grace of God. Jacques Maritain says that history progresses both in the direction of good and in the direction of evil, all at the same time. In spite of the demonic forces which are pervasive throughout the world, the City of God will eventually destroy the City of Man. Genuine social progress results from this historical process.

One may contend that social progress can be achieved even more vigorously in non-Christian countries such as Japan. We cannot ignore this historical reality. Yet such materialistic progress without a firm Christian foundation can only result in national calamities as we so vividly witnessed in the outcome of Japanese industrial and military growth in the prewar years. No society can make genuine social progress without engaging in an unceasing battle against individual and institutionalized sin.

Inasmuch as there is "no reason to expect any change in unredeemed human nature while human life goes on earth,"[44] we cannot perpetuate history without the grace of God. At times, Christians get discouraged with the slow tempo of the growth of God's Kingdom, but the biblical promise on the final outcome is unmistakably clear. Small as he was, David defeated Goliath. A small group of the early Christians—mostly poor and illiterate social outcasts—defeated the mighty Roman Empire. True social progress comes from our prayer, "Thy will be done on earth as it is in heaven," and from our efforts to bring "Thy Kingdom" into the world.

Small in number and opposed by formidable forces, we Asian Christians should be ready to suffer in evangelizing our societies. But hope is with us. C. V. Gheorghiu, the author of *The Twenty-Fifth Hour*, observes: "The downfall of technocracy in the West will be followed by a rebirth of human and spiritual values. This great light will probably come from the East, from Asia. Not from Russia. It is the Orient that will conquer this technocracy of the West."[45] Certainly the East will kindle light anew even in the West; but contrary to what many Western ideologies predict, it will not be a light of Asian traditionalism, but the very light that the West has been abandoning—the biblical teachings of Christianity. Probably, and very hopefully, the Chris-

tianization of Asian cultures may goad the West into rediscovering the spiritual heritages of her past.

With our goal the realization of the Kingdom of God in
our lands, we Asians must first dethrone nature—not, of
course, in the same manner the West is doing, but in the
manner that the Bible tells us. Instead of destroying nature
and disrupting the ecological milieu of human life with the
lethal threat of pollutants, we should learn how to manage it
for the glory of God, the Creator of all things. This concept
of stewardship can become the spiritual foundation of our
business ethics.

Secondly, we must reconstruct our relations with science
and technology. In the West, as Gerald Sykes points out,
"man rushes first to save by technology, then to be saved
from it."[46] We Asians, in the process of modernization,
must learn how to humanize technology so that instead of
shaping ourselves into its image we should be able to reshape it according to our humane ideals. Without this spiritual foundation, any further progress of science will be
meaningless, meaningless in the sense that it, like Frankenstein's Monster, will turn against us. True science and
true religion are twin sisters, and we cannot exclude one
from another; but they are far from being equals, for religion has been the matrix of all other values that man
creates.

With this spiritual aura, we must thirdly reconstruct the
moral fibre of our society. Without the faith that God is the
Father of all men, we cannot regard other human beings as
our brothers; and by the same token, without this spiritual
foundation of the equality of men, moral ideals, however
noble, will simply disintegrate and die. The citizens of the
City of God, in response to His call, will engage in a perpetual struggle against their sinful natures which pull them
morally downward and will try to be merciful, pure in
heart, courageous, self-controlled, and kind. These are the
virtues required for a sane moral society. But above all else,
Christian morality is based upon the *agape* love Christ

showed us by taking the pain of the cross on our behalf.

While living on earth, Christians cannot become morally perfect. We cannot free ourselves from the dialectical tension arising from the gap between the biblical ideals of God's Kingdom and the changing condition of our daily life, between loyalty to God and loyalty to our nation, between devotion to God and service to the world. But contradiction is a basic element of human existence, and tensions in our minds can be harmonized if we fix our goal to the Kingdom of God.

In more specific terms, Harold Dewolf writes how we can live for this transcendental goal in a transient world by the following principles: 1) The principle of consistency in which every Christian ought to will to be consistent in his intentions; 2) the principle of personal conscience, for every Christian ought to make decisions in accordance with the ideals his conscience acknowledges; 3) the principle of foresight in that every Christian ought to look ahead to see the foreseeable consequences of his actions; 4) the principle of the best possible, by which every Christian ought to will the best possible values in the total situation; 5) the principle of social gain by which every Christian ought to subordinate his gain for the happiness of the majority; and 6) the principle of ideal community by which every Christian ought to choose all of his values in loyalty to his ideals of what the whole community should become.[47]

All in all, by trying to live for God's Kingdom the life of a Christian transcends both individualism and collectivism and soars far above these secular ideologies. To identify Christianity with individualism or collectivism is not biblical, for our beliefs can encompass both and also rise far above them. The City of God is made up of those who accept Christ as their personal Savior, thereby letting Him live in their spirits; but these individuals can perfect themselves only as God's grace enables them to work for their fellowmen for His glory. In so doing, Christians—as followers of the same Lord—must collectively seek to realize the

Kingdom of God in their society. Although seemingly paradoxical, it is a profound truth that Christians are individualistic and collectivistic at the same time with no confusion in their minds because God's Kingdom includes them and transcends them.

4. CHRISTIAN FORMULA AS TESTED BY HISTORY

How can we then authenticate belief that the biblical teachings on historical progress are all-creative? Can we verify them with historical evidences? Although no ready-made answer for this question is available, we may make a cursory survey of the Christian influence upon the modernization of Western civilization as a case study.

Among the twenty-one civilizations that Arnold Toynbee enumerates, Western civilization was the only one which had made a decisive break with the nature-dominated ways of traditional life, eventually giving birth to modernization. The question as to how this was possible remains, even today, a historical enigma, a riddle for which, despite the laborious and voluminous works of the past few centuries, no simplistic answers can be found. The causes and effects of such a gigantic historical change are lost in the labyrinth of the past, making it utterly impossible to trace and pinpoint the original impulses of the event.

Theories of climate, topography, race, and diet are not convincing. The climate, land forms, and other environmental characteristics of Europe were not uniquely better than other parts of the world, nor did Europeans have uniquely superior racial qualities. The dialectic determinisms of Hegel and Marx failed in explaining why the West became the first fruit of modernization, for their theories were universal in nature.

In recent times, more sophisticated hypotheses concerning this question have appeared. David McClelland of Harvard University argues that the birth of modernization in the West presumes "the existence of a way of thinking that leads men to behave in a particularly energetic way—a mental virus which psychologists call the 'need for achievement.' '' For instance, he finds a large amount of this need for achievement in early Greek literature, in English popular literature of the sixteenth century, and in Spanish literature of the same century.[48] But he is not explicit on the point as to where the original impulse of this need for achievement came from. Alexander Gershenkron, an economic historian, suggests the theory of substitutability by pointing out the fact that credit creation by banks and public tax systems during the Renaissance period stimulated the social growth of the West.[49] Nevertheless, he too is ambiguous.

Instead of dwelling upon these endless and seemingly fruitless arguments, we must look at the question from a different angle, so as to find out what had constituted the spiritual milieu of the West and enabled Western civilization to become so dynamic and forward-looking. At this point, no one can question the overwhelming influence of Christianity upon the formation of the Western mind, which exteriorized itself in the heritage of Western civilization. With unswerving religious beliefs, Western man externalized his internal faith in his personal life, in his society, in his political institutions, in his legal systems, and in his social norms.

Suppose that there had never been Christianity in the West. Suppose that Western people had never heard of the Gospel. Suppose that they had never read the Bible. Suppose that they had believed in Hinduism, or Buddhism, or Taoism, or Confucianism, or Shamanism, or Shintoism. If so, would there have been Dante, Chaucer, Milton, and Tennyson in literature? Would there have been da Vinci, Michelangelo, Rubens, and Millet in painting? Would there have been Bach, Handel, Beethoven in music? Would there have been Bramante, Palladio, Wren, and de Brosse in architecture? Without Christianity, would there have been the institutionalization of such lofty ideals as liberty and equality in the West?

Already, in the early twentieth century, Max Weber, writing his monumental work *Protestant Ethic and the Spirit of Capitalism*, expounded the theory that the West had the seeds of modernity in Calvinism, especially in the Calvinistic ethical teachings which, with its theology of predestination, reinvigorated the practical Christian virtues such as calling, self-discipline, asceticism, stewardship, and hard work in social life.[50] Looking back beyond the Reformation period, Arnold Toynbee, on the other hand, maintained that the seeds of modernity had in fact been growing in the monastery, for in the Benedictine Rules we find many of the moral virtues, such as the sanctification of manual labor, that eventually became the backbone of Western ethics.[51] Furthermore, in *The Jews and Modern Capitalism*, Werner Sombart strongly maintained that the economic practice and social attitude associated with Judaism had been the primary factor for the birth of modern capitalism.[52]

These theories run counter to the prevailing intellectual climate of the West. Criticism of these theories comes from two main sources: namely, the unworldly ultraconservative Christians and the secular thinkers who still dwell in the eighteenth century Enlightenment tradition. Let us now examine these criticisms.

From the time of the early church, many thought that Christianity, standing above and beyond the mundane world, had nothing to do with secular civilization. Tertullian, for one, was against everything lying outside of the church, insisting that the "world" was opposed to Christianity. He was against Greek culture, Greek philosophy, Roman traditions, and Roman thought, and condemned them as things of absolutely no value.[53] Today, many pious other-worldly Christians tend to isolate themselves from direct involvement in social affairs. They say that the church is not of the world. They discourage Christian youth from becoming involved in politics. They believe that the

Christian life has nothing to do with worldly affairs, including business. Business is morally bad for it is geared to
making money—the source of all evils. If any Christian
takes this position, the Weberian thesis is totally wrong.

Next is the criticism from the left, the radical anti-
Christian thinkers who maintain that Christianity impedes
social progress. They often quote the story of Galileo who
was tried by the church for his new scientific discovery.
Karl Marx flatly said that "religion is the opium of the
people." Friedrich Nietzsche, with his conviction in the
"will to power," condemned Christianity as a religion of
"slave morals." Today, George Bataille slanders Christianity in more fierce terms: "This ethics is less an answer to
our ardent desires for reaching a summit than a bolt that
shuts us off from these desires."[54]

I concede that these two criticisms have some merit.
Other scholarly responses to the Weber thesis made by F.
Rachfall, R. H. Tawney, Winthrop Hudson, H. M.
Robertson, Amintore Farfani, and Albert Hyma—in support, in opposition, and in supplementation—also have
many important points. As the unworldly Christians warn
us, Christians must not become unduly "this-worldly." As
the unsympathetic anti-Christians clamor, the church as a
human organization has produced many adverse, undesirable effects upon human history. Many critical scholars
argue that saying capitalism was born of Calvinism is
simplistic.

What I propose here is, therefore, not to be dogmatic in
one way or the other, but to review the historical role of
Christianity in a balanced view, and then compare the
merits and demerits of Christianity to those other religions
in Asia. How then did Christianity give vitality to the birth
and growth of Western civilization? What then is the present relation between Christianity and Western civilization?

What the Germanic barbarians learned from the Church
as they wandered throughout the declining Roman Empire
was 1) to give up their primitive naturecentric views of the

world which were riddled with superstitions; 2) to avoid the danger of falling into anthropocentric views of man which had been prevalent among some Greco-Roman philosophers; and 3) to embrace the theocentric *Weltanshauung* of Christianity. The so-called Middle Ages were not "middle" in any sense, for the period was in actuality the "beginning" of Western civilization.

The Christian church became, in myth as well as in fact, the womb of the rising Western civilization, for during the early Middle Ages the Germanic barbarians acquired the biblical concept of God, nature, man, and history. Therefore, the desacralization of nature was possible. With their new faith in the Creator, they too could "subdue" the earth as the Bible commanded. Also, in this new spiritual milieu, anthropocentrism had no room to grow, for Western man could not exult about himself regardless of what he achieved. Always fallible to sin—anger, covetousness, envy, gluttony, lust, pride, sloth, etc.—man could not get rid of his consciousness of guilt, which was often carried to excessive extremes. Penance was the source of true individualism, not egoism, which could balance itself between human rights and individual responsibilities.

As time went by, as the situation became somewhat stabilized, a few small-scale renaissances were attempted to revive the secular heritages of Greco-Roman civilization. However, these renaissances should not be construed as an intellectually secular movement against Christianity; but rather, they should be interpreted as an attempt to integrate the cultural remains of Greco-Roman civilization into the Christian world-view. What I emphatically stress here is a new interpretation of the Renaissance—an interpretation which runs counter to the version traditionally accepted among Western historians. In his celebrated work, *The Civilization of the Renaissance in Italy*, Jacob Bruckhardt, for instance, maintained that the Italian Renaissance was a sudden outburst of intellectual energy—largely secular in nature—which the Italian genius fashioned after the heritages of Greco-Roman culture.[55] Other historians have claimed that it resulted from the direct outgrowth of Moslem civilization which came to the West through Spain.

Of course, in the paintings, sculptures, architectures, and humanistic writings of the Renaissance period we do find the strong, pervasive concept of *Humanitas*. At first glance it appears that the whole movement was an anthropocentric rebellion against Christian theocentrism. But can an age change so drastically and precipitately? To regard Petrarch, Boccaccio, Michelangelo, and Leonardo da Vinci as anti-Christian would be analogous to the misconception that Galileo and Newton were atheists. True, they did laugh about priests and saints. But their anticlericalism was directed against the organized church which, increasingly made callous by its hardened ecclesiastical tradition, had drifted away from the biblical path.

What Renaissance humanists consequently derided was not the Gospel itself, but church structure, tradition, and practice. To me, an Asian who can read Western history with emotional detachment about historical events, what the Renaissance intellectuals shouted was, therefore, an outcry for the spiritual regeneration of the West, a rebellion which remained, by and large, within the Hebrew-Christian framework. In spite of his carping criticism against the church, Thomas More, for instance, remained a true Roman Catholic until his tragic death. In a way, judging from its long-term effects, the Renaissance paved the way for the coming of the Reformation just as John the Baptist paved the way for Jesus.

Despite their shortcomings and mistakes, reformers like Martin Luther, John Calvin, John Knox, and others tried to do their best, even at the risk of facing death, to regenerate, purify, and revitalize the biblical principles and doctrines. In their own ways, they succeeded in achieving their aims. But for this biblical foundation, the birth of modernization could not have been possible.

Of course, I am aware of the danger of the dogmatic assertion that Christianity alone gave birth to modernization. To
simplify the multifarious factors of modernization in such a
monistic generalization can be misleading. If Christianity is
invariably to produce modernization, why then did not the
Greek Orthodox Church and the Coptic Church do the
same? We must not in any sense disparage the important
contribution that the heritages of Greco-Roman civilization
made to the rise of the modern West. Nor can we depreciate
the crucial roles played by the middle class, nationalism,
rationalism, humanism, overseas expansion, scientific
progress, and ironically enough, the dynastic rivalries and
wars in bringing forth what we call modernity. Yet, com-
paratively speaking, the revival of the biblical principles in
religious life gave far stronger stimuli to the rise of modernity than the aggregation of all other forces.

To be more specific, William Woodruff wrote in *The Impact of Western Man* of the Christian influence upon the
birth of modernity as follows: 1) "The materialism of Christianity," the stress on man's earthly as well as his heavenly
lot; 2) the concept that "man is a unity of body and spirit,"
and Christian redemption is not simply redemption of the
spirit but the resurrection of the body as well; 3) the idea
that Christianity is "the religion of hope looking forward to
the second coming of Christ and the establishment of the
kingdom of God on earth"; 4) the "Christian idea of a common humanity which helps to explain the European attitude towards commerce"; and 5) "the new trust placed in
the power of the individual in place of the older forms of
established authority, such as the family, tribe, clan,
church, or feudal system."[56]

In a way, the birth of modernization in the West was
brought about in a most paradoxical way. Christianity as
the eternal *Logos* had trained the Western people for nearly
a millenium to bear this fruit; but precisely at the moment
of transformation, the church as an organized institution,
already aged by its callous tradition, stood against the

changes which biblical principles had effectuated. Here
again we see a profound truth. The spiritual lethargy of the
church made people yearn after the grace of God, and this
spiritual reawakening, contrary to common sense, spurred
material progress. People cannot make material progress by
simply being materialistic because it results from spiritual
innovation. "Seek ye first the kingdom of God, and his
righteousness, and all these things shall be added unto
you" (Matthew 6:33).

A word of caution is necessary here. If every man becomes unduly spiritual, as we see in the present situation in
India, society will be defunct or at best retrogressive. If, on
the other hand, everyone becomes unduly materialistic, society will become an arena of brutish struggle. But the
theocentrism of the Bible avoids these two pitfalls. By loving God, man has to love his fellow beings. By his efforts to
realize the Kingdom of God, to ameliorate social ills, and to
realize God's righteousness and love in human society, man
may improve society, thereby contributing to historical
progress. To a large extent, social progress has been made
not by revolutionaries who, with their man-made
ideologies, try to remold society in their own image—but
by the true believers who, with their detachment from the
mundane world, endeavor to realize God's will on earth.

At this point, however, one point must be made absolutely clear. In no way do I imply that Christianity and
Western civilization have become one inseparable unity as
the mistaken concept of Christendom holds. This is far from
being the actual case. Judaism gave rise to Judaic civilization, but those two were by no means identical. Time and
again we read in the Old Testament the warnings of
prophets against the iniquity of Jewish people who fell far
short of the Mosaic laws. So is the case with the relationship
between Christianity and Western civilization. Western
civilization may decay, decline, and disintegrate, but the
ideals and principles which inspired it can remain unmolested and unscarred, and may germinate a new civiliza-

tion elsewhere. Christianity transcended the disintegration of Roman civilization and then started developing a new civilization in the West. Western civilization may follow the historical course of Roman civilization, but Christianity will not die with it. Arnold Toynbee writes concerning this historical truth: "If religion is a chariot, it looks as if the wheels on which it mounts towards heaven may be the periodic downfalls of civilization on earth. It looks as if the movement of civilizations may be cyclic and recurrent, while the movement of religion may be on a single continuous upward line."[57] Now, with this broad premise in mind, let us view briefly the relationship between Christianity and Western civilization.

Modernization has been a complex phenomenon. It has been regarded as the sum total of political democratization, intellectual rationalization, economic industrialization, social equalization, mass education, and a myriad of other changes which have characterized modern life.

For many centuries, probably up until the early twentieth century, optimists praised modernization as the vehicle by which utopia will be achieved on earth. Certainly it appeared so. Among the many splendid creations that the modern West has made, one most outstanding achievement is the conquest of nature through the development of science and technology. Never before has man become so powerful, so affluent, and so limitless in his control of natural forces as he is in today's West. What man can do by dint of science and technology simply dazzles one, and the material progress resulting from this development defies the imagination.

However, in the long course of the modernization process something has gone wrong. Amid material affluence, Western man has become unduly grumpy, grouchy, spiritually indigent, and hypochondriac. Nature has been excessively polluted, and ecological problems arising in the industrially advanced countries are threatening the very existence of man on earth. The dangers of social breakdown, class war, racial conflict, and political calamity are increasingly evident in the West. Now pessimists foresee not only the "decline of the West," but also the eschatological end of the whole world. Why?

The reasons are too numerous to mention. But one commonly accepted diagnosis is that the basic cause of today's crisis in the West lies in the imbalance of life—the imbalance between material life and spiritual life. So engrossed in material progress, Western man seems to have forgotten his spiritual foundations and civilization has become disequilibriated and crippled. The majority of Western people are, in Herbert Marcuse's often quoted phrase, "one dimensional." However, I believe that the real cause lies in a deeper dimension, the dimension of man's mind. This is to say that Western civilization is losing its spiritual foundation. Nicolas Berdyaev, a noted Russian philosopher, observes a danger inherent in the relationship between religion and civilization:

> Culture develops a tendency to disintegrate in its religious and spiritual foundations and to repudiate its own symbolism. And this fact reveals the fatal dialectic interest in culture. For at a certain state of its existence, it begins to doubt and criticize the premises upon which it rests. It prepares its own destruction by separating itself from its source. It passes from the "organic" to the "critical" stage of its existence.[58]

The West has drifted away from the Christian worldview, away from Christian ethics and values. The churches are still there with many churchgoers involved in doing good, but the spiritual vitality of religious life is seriously lacking.

One widely and uncritically accepted theory is that modern science has eroded the authority of God. There is no doubt that this theory has some validity. As La Place said, "Modern science has found the hypothesis of God less and less necessary."[59] Modern physics, with its exploration into an infinitely multiplex universe, has given rise to doubts about the biblical creation theory, and new discoveries in paleontology cast doubt on the biblical narration of the Garden of Eden. Charles Darwin's biological theory of evolution has eroded the traditional belief in the Providence of God working in human history. Freudian psychoanalysis explains away the Christian concept of sin in terms of an unconscious substream of the human psyche. This process of de-Christianization, plus many other factors, have produced multifarious results.

The biblical definition of the relationship between God and man has been virtually, if not completely, reversed, with man dethroning God and enthroning himself in the position of his Creator. The process of demythologization which originally directed against nature goes on against God. Even from the Bible, anything we cannot understand in terms of today's scientific knowledge is eliminated in the name of demythologization. Nothing remains mysterious. In the end, the very existence of God is being expelled from Western man's life and thought. God is now reduced to the idealization of man's yearning to be holy and just.

In retrospect, when deism in the eighteenth century challenged the revealed beliefs of Christianity, not many people took it seriously. When Jean Paul discoursed on the "dead Christ" and proclaimed his atheism openly, saying "there is no God," in his *Siebenkas* published in 1796, no Christian apologetics paid attention to him.[60] But by the next century, liberal theology, with its semi-scientific methods investigation using mainly philology, made phenomenal headway in the form of higher criticism. The trend against revelation culminated in Nietzsche's declaration that "God is dead." "God is on the border of life, constantly being pushed back," wrote Dietrich Bonhoeffer, the tragic German theologian, "because the West has been proceeding toward a time of no religion at all." Or to put it more realistically, "even those who honestly describe themselves as 'religious' do not in the least act up to it."[61] Today Gabriel Vahanian says that "it is not sacrilegious to speak of the death of God. After all, the concept of God is a cultural concept, and God often is nothing other than some sort of constant accessory of culture."[62]

Of course, the rise of the Neo-Orthodox Theology under the influence of Karl Barth and others has swung the extremely liberalizing theological trend back to the middle, but it could not reinstate God in the center of Western life. On the other hand, the religious bigotry of ultraconservatives who utterly refuse to use reason—a God-given gift to man—in applying biblical principles to our ever-changing historical conditions, and who condemn anything and everything produced by modern science and technology, have little influence upon the course of history. In the end, what is left in the West is a gigantic spiritual interregnum—a great spiritual void.

Second, in this spiritual interregnum, man simply enthrones himself in the place of God. Perhaps unintentionally, modern humanism has rendered its service to the birth of anthropocentrism, although, in my view, these two are quite different. Unlike Renaissance humanism, modern anthropocentrism claims that man has an autonomous existence and derives his being from no one else, depends upon no one else, and belongs to no one else. Man is a self-sufficient microcosmos. Dietrich Bonhoeffer wrote, "Man has learned to cope with all questions of importance without recourse to God as a working hypothesis. In questions concerning science, art, and even ethics, this has become an understood thing which one scarcely dares to tilt at any more."[63] History has come to bear a new meaning. It now has no divine sanction. Nor does it unfold the divine plan of God. It has become purely a human history, the story of man's splendid achievements. The secularized form of history does not, however, negate the linear concept of man's progression in time; it too has become secularized. In other words, man finds the meaning of his life in historical time which is believed to be progressing, steadily and rapidly, toward a utopia on earth. The expectation of peace and justice through man's efforts replaces the expectation of the Kingdom of God.

In his anthropocentricity directed against God, modern Western man has relied upon reason to the point of deifying it. We know now that Reason deified has guided man nowhere except to wars, violence, and irrationality. All the scientific progress that Western man has achieved under the guidance of Reason has reduced him to a meaningless being. Darwinism reduced him to an animal, Freudianism to a sex impulse, and modern psychology to a power-craving machine. The age of Reason has driven man to nihilistic despair. Ernst Cassirer laments on the situation, saying:

> Man's claim to being the center of the universe has lost its foundation. Man is placed in an infinite space in which his being seems to be a single and vanishing point. He is surrounded by a mute universe. The Copernican system became one of the strongest instruments of philosophical agnosticism and skepticism.[64]

Third, against this dismal background Western man, with almost frantic zeal, has tried to find a political and economic panacea in terms of the suggestions made by sociopolitical ideologies. In his anxiety to escape from the utter futility of a meaningless existence, he, as John Hallowell points out, is tempted to "give up his most priceless heritage—his freedom—to any man who even promises deliverance from insecurity" and is willing to "put his faith in the most absurd doctrines."[65] But thus far, these secular gospels have not, and cannot, eradicate evil—the source of nihilism—from man's existence. Liberalism, by denying the reality of evil, ascribes it to faulty political institutions and Marxism to the capitalistic mode of production. In a most paradoxical way, both of these diametrically opposing ideologies agree on one point: human nature is essentially good. They see only the ripples on the surface, without touching the depth of the problem. Because of this naiveté, they have failed miserably in leading the world to a man-made utopia.

Nihilism expresses itself not only in the dispirited, despondent mood of the ghettos, but also in the idealism of upper- or middle-class youth. It is pervasive, not only in the mirthless, atrabilious writings of modern literature, but also in the madness of the modern arts. Violent mass actions and terrorist activities are, more often than not, motivated by nihilism and much less by sanguine idealism. The atheistic existentialism of Sartre and others, which declares the senselessness, forlornness, and meaninglessness of modern life, is also fed by and is feeding nihilism.

Fourth, suddenly Western man has found that his civilization is no longer anthropocentric, but technocentric. The industrial systems of the highly advancd societies have become so complex and gigantic that in the end they control human beings, putting the cart before the horse. The relationship between principal and auxiliary has completely, or almost completely, turned the other way around, making man subservient to his own creation. Technology is more than something mechanical. In addition to mechanical engineering, technology today deals with planetary engineering, global engineering, biological engineering, social engineering, political engineering, and even human engineering.

A popular descriptive label for the psychic state of the Western mind in this age of technology is "the Counter-Enlightenment." No longer is he the lord of history. Trapped by impersonal forces beyond his control, man has become a stranger wandering aimlessly in the historical plane. Arnold Toynbee passed a judgment on the present state of Western civilization, saying that the West is now passing on "from the symptoms of breakdown to the symptoms of disintegration." Ortega y Gasset wrote:

We live at a time when man believes himself fabulously capable of creation, but he does not know what to create. Lord of all things, he is not lord of himself. He feels lost amid his own abundance. With more means at his disposal, more knowledge, more technique than ever, it turns out that the world today goes the same way as the worst of worlds that have been: it simply drifts.[66]

This does not mean that Pied Pipers are entirely nonexistent in today's West. On the contrary, to our amazement many "social engineers" are busy presenting their blueprints, mostly based upon the optimistic extension of today's scientific-technological progress. In recent years, especially after the establishment of Conseil de Furturibles in 1961, the futuristic projections of such scholars as Bertrand de Jouvenel, Michael Young, Daniel Bell, Herman Khan, and Dennis Gabor have fermented polemics on the prospects of the world in general, and of the West in particular. Despite the divergent opinions spanning a wide spectrum between optimism and pessimism, they echo Albert Einstein's pithy epigram that "a new type of thinking is essential if mankind is to survive and move to a higher level." How then can we formulate such a new type of thinking?

If we are to avoid the impending atomic Armageddon, we must create a new spiritual milieu in which "nation shall not lift swords against nation." If we are to realize such a milieu, most futurists agree that the ideals of humanism must henceforth be the ultimate goals of mankind. Science, technology, mega-machines, mega-organizations, values, and norms should be rehumanized. In lieu of the hitherto widely accepted idea that the clash of opposites is the very condition of progress, we must instill a new concept that peace can only be realized through the harmony of conflict and contrast on the basis of a pan-consciousness. All these sound wonderful, too plausible to be in anyway refuted. But how can we create such a humane spiritual milieu? No one can deny that the institutionalized evils prevailing in our world—wars, mass-murders, neo-colonialism, racism, and dictatorship—are mere superficial phenomena of the evil, not the evil itself. But nothing, including humanitarian and humanistic education, has rectified the evil tendencies of men. Westerners, so proud of what they have achieved, have become self-complacent, self-righteous, and less and less sincere in admitting their sinfulness. Sociopolitical ideologies such as liberalism, socialism, and Communism simply ignore this most persistent of problems as if it does not exist. Instead, socialism and Communism have recently gained considerable political influence in such Western countries as Italy, Portugal, Spain, and France. Since a real renewal of Christianity in the West is highly unlikely, writes a Western social critic, "the end of the Western culture is more than likely."[67]

The present crisis in the West poses a serious question to all Asian nations. In our efforts to modernize our societies, should we try to emulate the West? Or should we return to our own past? What then is the best sociopolitical ideology suitable to our future? Is it liberal democracy? Is it Communism? Is it socialism? Is it nationalism? Is it cosmopolitanism? What should be the spiritual basis for our "new thinking?"

3

Beyond Sociopolitical Ideologies

As has been emphatically stressed in the previous chapters, the contradictory syndromes confronting us in today's Asia cannot be synthesized by autonomous powers inherent within themselves or by some impersonal historical laws. It must be done by the consorted, dedicated efforts of people to achieve some common spiritual goals. Spiritual endeavor cannot remain irrelevant to material progress, for spirit manifests itself through matter.

With regard to the eternal spiritual goal that mankind should seek to realize in historical time, Matthew 6:33 is very explicit: "Seek ye first the kingdom of God, and his righteousness, and all these things shall be added unto you." This verse tells us the paradoxical truth that if an individual—let alone a society—becomes solely materialistic and seeks nothing but economic gains, it will become his tower of Babel and, instead of offering happiness will eventually ruin him. On the other hand, if he seeks to realize God's Kingdom in every realm of his life, he may enjoy both material blessings and spiritual happiness without sacrificing one for another.

Inasmuch as the City of God exists as the spiritual goal of Christians in the future, not as a historical event of the past, it goads us to be forward-looking and progressive, rather than backward-looking and retrogressive. Consequently, this religious goal inspires people to be productive in a myriad of social, economic, technological, political, and cultural changes, making a historical *Aufheben* possible. Let us now compare the concept of the Kingdom of God with other secular ideologies.

1. BEYOND DEMOCRACY AND COMMUNISM

Today most Asian societies are rapidly becoming *politicized*. With the tempo of modernization moving as speedily as it has in the postwar era, political power—the leading force of all the changes we experience—becomes limitlessly expansive and dominates almost every aspect of people's lives. The government regulates economic changes, establishes educational systems, creates the cultural milieu, and even interferes in people's sexual lives by telling them, through the policy of birth control, how many children are suitable for each household. Being so exhaustively all-inclusive, political power often seeks to control human minds, thereby creating intricate antagonistic issues in its relation with the spiritual power of the church. No matter how unworldly and disinterested in secular affairs we may become, we cannot remain *apolitical*.

Beneath the complicated political issues confronting us in today's Asia is a fundamental question: Is there a political structure which Christians can support? Many Christians, without giving much thought to the complexities underlying this apparently simple inquiry, jump to the popularly accepted conclusion that we Asian Christians must be as strongly in favor of democracy as we are against Communist rule. Many of us blindly identify ourselves with liberal democracy and regard socialism as something antithetical to Christianity.

The problem gets even more aggravated as we see the diverse forms of government presently existing in today's Asia. There are as many species of regimes in Asia as there are nations; they are so varied that it is well-nigh impossible to classify them into a few simplistic categories like democratic, Communist, or socialist. Some variance has become evident even among the Communist states. The

Maoist state of Red China, for instance, set itself miles apart from the government of the Soviet Union; nor are the Communist regimes of North Korea and of North Vietnam identical. Even in the non-Communist Asian countries, democracy exists in name only, with varying degrees of authoritarianism among them. One-man rule has become a political fad among the Asian states.

In this complex but pathetic situation, the range of our political options is extremely limited. We have difficulty finding any polity to our liking.

Regardless of what forms of Communist political systems presently exist in Asia, we Christians cannot support any one of them. The Gospel has nothing in common with the inhumane brutality of the Communist states. Our Christian beliefs cannot be reconciled with Communist methods of extirpating political enemies and of superimposing their prefabricated blueprints upon the people. Furthermore, to me at least, Communism presents itself as a modernized, sophisticated version of *naturecentrism* because it has developed its ideological dogmas in the mistaken belief that matter is the essence of all beings.

Nor can we jump to the conclusion that liberal democracy is basically biblical in origin. With no sense of disparaging its immensely great merits as compared to other forms of government, I do not select liberal democracy as our political choice because it derives its ideals from anthropocentrism—man as the center of the universe with a limitless capability to perfect himself and his society in historical time. In this very fact of placing its basic faith in man's perfectability lies the fallacy of liberal political thought, for the optimistic concept of human nature and the Idea of Progress—the two pillars of liberalism—are, at best, the anachronistic residues of Enlightenment philosophy. Without God's grace, man's efforts to steer his own historical course unavoidably end up producing adverse effects perilous to his own existence.

Likewise, socialism is an inadequate political philosophy

based upon anthropocentrism. It, too, believes quite naively in the infallibility of human reason as the sole guide for man's destiny in the future. Socialism assumes that human beings are so reasonable as to cooperate in social progress without serious discord, so unselfish as to engage in material production obediently without creating serious disharmony, and so altruistic as to divide the fruits of production equally without resulting in inimical feelings. But in reality, socialist polity does not function unless, like the system of government in Soviet Russia, it uses a considerable amount of violence as a means of coercing people.

Nor can we opt for any other existing polity in today's Asia. Most Asian governments are corrupt, with elections rigged and the freedom of people oppressed. Martial law and national emergency decrees, suspending the fundamental civil rights and liberties of people, are indiscriminately promulgated. Anyone opposing such undemocratic measures is subject to arrest, internment, and extremely harsh sentences, perhaps even death. Irate and enraged, young dissidents often express their discontent by staging demonstrations, only to meet more inhumane measures of coercion.

As Christians we find that all existing governments are in one way or the other tainted by sin. Usually government is a political tool of the ruling elite, whether it be a dominant class or a party or a military-industrial complex. Popular sovereignty has proven itself to be a modern myth which exists only in people's imaginations, because the masses—incapable of controlling complicated political mechanisms—are ruthlessly manipulated and exploited by the ruling elite. Using oppressive and repressive measures, the Communist regimes are more expressive than subtler non-Communist authoritarian governments. But as Romans 3:23 states, "For all have sinned, and come short of the glory of God."

As Christians, therefore, we cannot claim that a certain form of government is superior to others. So long as human nature, which exteriorizes itself in politics, remains sinful no perfect government can be realized in historical time.

I think that Christian realism, in contrast to other political thought-systems, presupposes two seemingly contradictory concepts of man as the theoretical foundation of civil polity: Man as the image of God with inherent dignity and all accompanying inherent rights, and man as an incorrigible sinner always fallible to sin and corruption. In this image of God lies man's capability in planning, organizing, and directing his social and political affairs. In addition, the fact of God's creating man and woman to live together in harmony inspires us to work collectively in society, influencing history by way of subduing nature, taming natural forces, and utilizing the powers of nature for human welfare. But the Bible realistically tells us that human beings could not remain in the original state of happiness, for by rebelling against God they committed sin and fell from His grace.

This duality of man can be understood in paradoxical terms. The fact of our being created in God's image enables us to create a civil polity, and the fact of our being so sinful necessitates a civil government. For these two conflicting and contradictory reasons the government has come to exist in history. Because of God's image in man, the government can work for human welfare; and because of man's sinful nature, it must vigilantly safeguard law and order in society so that anarchy and chaos may not prevail.

In Christian thought, government cannot be an end in itself. Like other social organizations, it is a means to an end, the end of serving people. By maintaining freedom and justice in human affairs, it creates a political milieu in which people may freely develop their potentialities. All in all, government exists for two seemingly contradictory roles: the promotion of human welfare, and the punishment of evildoers. Christians can bear any form of polity so long as it, as ordained by God, maintains righteousness in society and genuinely strives to give people welfare, security, and freedom. To identify Christianity, therefore, with any one type of polity as against others can be regarded as un-biblical. After all, the Kingdom of God transcends all secular political ideologies.

At this point, difficult problems arise. The fact remains that the rulers in power are as much prone to sinning as the ruled. Or to put it more realistically, those in power and in influence are even more tempted to commit sins of pride and vanity. In proportion to the amount of power, people become increasingly proud, arrogant, profligate, and lascivious. Power inevitably corrupts. Sin decomposes any polity, be it democratic, socialistic, or Communistic. No human institution can be immune from it.

With this in mind, Christians should support the kind of government which, with a strong awareness of this duality of man, tries to safeguard itself from sinning, pursue social justice, and promote people's welfare.

What then must we do when, contrary to our expectation, a government turns out to be unjust, corrupt, and oppressive as most Asian governments have become these days? Many Asian authoritarian rulers behave as though they fear no authority above them. They amass fortunes by abusing political power and stamp out the voice of conscience with brutal suppression. With blood on their hands, they move quickly to strike deadly blows against anyone who dares voice opposing opinions. Blinded by sin, haughty, and seeking vainglory in false self-righteousness, these dominant minorities try to make their political power limitless and omnipotent.

As followers of Christ, are we to remain in passive obedience? Are we to resort to nonresistance? Herein lies the dividing line between the moderates who advocate gradual change in politics and the radicals who vehemently insist upon taking political action. This division of opinion among Asian Christians today finds a historical precedent in Nazi Germany before World War II when the German church, in spite of its Protestant tradition stemming from the Reformation, failed to protest the rise of Hitler. By the time Hitler became so powerful and was about to drive the whole world into an Armageddon-like holocaust, the German ecclesiastical leaders were too debilitated, enervated, and languid to voice their opposition to him. In the end, men like Dietrich Bonhoeffer were unable to change the situation. We can cite many similar cases among the Soviet satellite nations in the postwar era.

When we view our present situation in the light of these historical precedents, we cannot regard "unworldliness" as a Christian virtue. Nor can we seclude ourselves in the hope of the Second Coming of Christ. What is urgently required of us is thoughtful actions, getting our hands dirty in political affairs, both individually and collectively. In our rapidly politicizing society, we cannot stand aloof from mundane affairs—the affairs which constantly affect our spiritual and physical life. Our faith in Christ must be translated into political action, if a situation so demands.

In North Korea and in Red China, no freedom of religious worship is allowed. No church exists officially. During the initial stage of the North-South talks in Korea, Kim Il Sung's uncle, Kang Yang Wuk—an ordained minister of the Korean Presbyterian Church, and chairman of the All People's Congress—was asked about the number of Christians still alive in North Korea. Kang Yang Wuk chuckled and said that no Christian churches existed in northern Korea because "American bombings during the Korean War destroyed all of them." Now, seeing the spectre of Leviathan in other Asian nations, we Asian Christians must try our best to save ourselves from evil, the evil of political totalitarianism.

If so, do we have to become revolutionaries and engage in subversive activities? Can we beautify and sublimate violence and use it as our means of struggle, as some Catholic priests in Latin America have done? Some Asian Christians seriously consider this the only option available now. They insist on taking violent action against governments, maintaining that a political power so deeply allied with the military cannot be dislodged by peaceful persuasion alone.

But I disagree. I don't think violence can be our answer. The overthrow of one government by violent means will, more than likely, complicate the situation beyond our control. If no spiritual revolution accompanies it, political revolution, coup, and counter-coup merely accelerate the vicious cycle of bloodshed and lead us nowhere. Through violent revolution, one mode of self-righteousness is only replaced by another form of self-righteousness. The overthrow of one tyranny might result in the establishment of another tyranny, sometimes even more vicious, as we saw in the military revolutions of the Asian countries in the early 1960s. Revolution breeds revolution, bloodshed more bloodshed. Violence cannot be eradicated by more violence; nor will the sinfulness of a society be rooted out by the elimination of those who happen to be in power. In Matthew 26, we read that Jesus, rebuking one of his disciples who drew his sword and struck at the High Priest's servant, disapproved the use of violence, saying, "They that take the sword shall perish with the sword."

Once we start to justify even a small amount of violence as something necessary and inevitable, there is no limit to such justification. How much violence is permissible to our Christian conscience? Undoubtedly, we cannot accept terrorist attacks; nor can we engage in guerrilla warfare against the power elite.

Instead, I think that what we must do as Christians is to uphold the torch of perpetual revolution, not in the manner of the Jacobins, but in the way of the ancient Jewish prophets. Changes in our society are not only necessary, but also imperative; and as long as both man and society are tainted by sin, we Christians cannot remain conservative. We must be revolutionaries as all the biblical saints were. What is the biblical way of reforming and transforming a sinful society?

Practically all the ancient prophets were men of strong social consciousness. Rebuking the powerful on behalf of the downtrodden, they endeavored in all possible ways to "seek judgment, relieve the opressed" (Isaiah 1:17). They could not bear to see the rich "grinding the faces of the poor." However, the Old Testament prophets did not, even when they could, lead political rebellions against the ruling monarchs after the manner of today's left-wing guerrilla leaders.

Nor did they remain silent in civil disobedience. Instead, in the name of God, they carried out perpetual spiritual revolution by both admonishing the kings and rebuking the sins of their people. Bearing the message of God, they spoke the truth adamantly and undauntedly, even at the risk of their lives. Take, for instance, the case of Elijah. King Ahab tried to kill him because of the message of God with which he admonished the king. Probably Elijah with his popularity could have led a successful political rebellion against Ahab, the unpopular king, and establish a new dynasty by crowning himself king or someone else as his puppet. But he did not do this. Knowing human nature well, Elijah apparently saw the futility of such a course in eradicating social injustice. He knew the war was to be waged perpetually. Hiding in the mountains and wandering in the wilderness, he continued to carry on that revolution.

Our Lord Jesus also did not tolerate the injustice prevailing in his time. He scolded the hypocritical life-style of the elite: "Ye are like whited sepulchres" (Matthew 23:27). On the other hand, when He saw the masses who followed Him He said, "I have compassion on the multitude" (Mark 8:2). Yet, despite such a great multitude following Him, Christ did not seek to establish a new Jewish state by starting a rebellion. His mission was, and still is, for the Kingdom of God. The road Jesus took was more tedious, more dangerous, and seemingly more unrewarding, than an outright popular rebellion.

By reasoning alone we may conclude that Jesus' method of opening new chapters in human history was totally useless in achieving any positive goals. In the end, He took up the cross, and everything seemed to be buried with Him in the grave. But He rose again, conquering not only the Roman Empire in historical time, but also the Satanic Empire beyond historical time.

Like the ancient Jewish prophets, we Asian Christians must love our society and our people so much that we should not be afraid of speaking the truth against the iniquities of the powerful ruling elite, even at the risk of endangering our own well-being. Individually, each one of us must emulate the life of Elijah in spite of the danger of taking up the cross as Jesus did. The church must take up the role of watchman, constantly vigilant against the evils erupting in our society. The church must be the guardian of freedom, because without it man can neither develop his potentiality nor fulfill himself. Without freedom no church as an organized body of Christians can prosper.

However, moving one step further beyond this negative struggle against the abuse of political power, we must develop Christian political thought in positive terms as well. What then is the best possible form of government?

This is a question which cannot be resolved by wishful thinking. The governmental structure of a given society changes almost continuously in the wake of cultural and economic changes. By the same token, it must be flexible enough to adapt itself to the rapidly changing historical conditions of the times. Gone is the concept that the less government the better. With the ever-accelerating tempo of historical change and with the ever-increasing demands of the people, government must be dynamic enough to take up the multiple roles of political enterprises.

If a government is going to be flexible in adapting itself to the changing times, but at the same time be unswerving in its goal of serving the people, Christian realism tells us that it must be based upon theocentrism, with God, not man, as the center of all political activities. Anthropocentric polity eventually turns against human rights, with the ruling elite becoming more and more capricious in its abuses of power. A theocentric polity works for human freedom, for the only tangible way of serving God is to serve people, especially those people who are downtrodden. Abraham Lincoln, for example, used to kneel before God at least once a day and confess his sins for not being able to serve Him as he should, and in this humility lay his greatness as a liberator of men and women.

What is most necessary for a good government is this theocentric spiritual milieu. A good democratic constitution can thrive only where both the rulers and the ruled seek to glorify God. If, on the contrary, the ruling elite aspire to be equal to God, the whole body politic turns into a diabolic force engulfing human rights, human freedom, and social progress. To ensure a good government, Christian realism demands a few specified conditions.

First, a government must institutionally safeguard itself from falling into corruption and collective sinning. Among the forms of government presently in existence, democratic polity has by far the best available safeguard mechanisms. The term of president or of any other high government officials must be limited to a few years, possibly not more than five years, with only two terms permitted for an individual. Even the American constitution did not have this provision until a constitutional amendment was put into effect in the mid-twentieth century. Whatever excuses he had, Franklin D. Roosevelt made a dire mistake in breaking the tradition established by George Washington of not running for a third term. It was fortunate for America that there still remained a residue of Puritan realism which reacted against this dangerous predecent.

Viewed in the light of this Christian realism, most Asian nations are now in serious political trouble because not only have practically all the highest government officials in the Asian countries, except possibly Japan, stayed in power longer than Christian realism would permit—they are trying to extend their terms of office indefinitely. Under these circumstances, no peaceful change of government appears to be in line; and as a consequence, Lord Acton's pithy adage proves itself a truism.

Secondly, if a government wants to remain sane, the power it wields must be divided, and the mechanism of checks and balances must be wisely devised. There is a popular misconception that Montesquieu was the first political thinker who conceived this idea of dividing power into three branches of government with checks and balances among them, but it is not historically valid. In England, by the time of the Stuart Restoration in 1660, the absolute monarchy, with all power placed in one person, was already a thing of the past. The Glorious Revolution of 1688 was "glorious" in the sense that it gave birth to the division of power among the monarchy (very soon, the prime minister) and the court and the parliament; therefore, what Montesquieu did in his famous *The Spirit of Law* in mid-eighteenth century France was to put this English system of government into a written form in systematic and logical order. But as a historian, I believe we can jump back further into human history and find its origin in the rise of the Jewish prophets who performed the role of checking the absolute power of the monarch. Also, in the Middle Ages the role of the pope in checking the power of the emperor and of the kings laid the foundation for the modern democratic division of power.

One may argue against my theory by pointing out the fact that in China and in Korea there was the system of the censors whose primary job was to admonish and reprimand the wrongdoings of the monarch. But the fact remains that the censors were government officials and at the mercy of the crown.

Viewed in the light of Christian realism, most Asian governments today are retrogressing to Oriental Despotism, to the tradition which can easily turn into autocracy. In most countries, the court has long ceased to be an independent branch of government and is incapable of checking the arbitrary power of the executive branch; and equally powerless is the parliament, which has virtually become a rubber stamp for what has already been decided by the executive. Some intellectual mouthpieces of the power elite try to justify this unhappy trend by saying that even in America the power of the presidency has become more influential than that of the Supreme Court and of Congress. But their sophistry has lost its persuasiveness since Watergate. As long as human nature remains as it is the political power of government must be divided, and a well-lubricated mechanism of checks and balances must function to safeguard the civil rights and liberty of the people.

Third, in order to be upright, a government must allow criticism and be tolerant of critical opinions. If any ruler accepts the fact of his sinful nature he should likewise acknowledge the fallibility of his political decisions and be open-minded towards different views. Without free public opinion there are bound to be hushed-up scandals in politics. The freedom of public opinion is an ever-renewing, ever-regenerating force which purifies the body politic.

This is directly related to the right of the people to know the truth, for the best way of arriving at truth is by the free competition of ideas. Here we see the primary importance of the free press. Despite its tendency toward sensationalism and commercialism, the free press is by far the best method for satisfying the public's right to know the truth. In the advanced societies of the West, the press has been regarded as the fourth branch of government. It is, therefore, the branch which, more than any other social organization, checks the abuses of the power elite.

Viewed in the light of freedom of expression most governments in Asia today have deviated far from the right path. Asian political leaders receive criticism as poorly as Ahab handled the rebukes of Elijah. They cannot tolerate even constructive criticism. Being so arrogant, so self-righteous, and so callous, they employ all the means within their reach to silence opinions different from theirs and stamp out political opposition thoroughly and without remorse. Newspapers are closed down without due process of law. Firms which used to support a newspaper by purchasing ad space are persuaded or compelled to discontinue that practice. With the press so relentlessly suppressed, most Asian societies have become intellectually blind, culturally moribund, and politically lethargic.

Fourth, if a government wants to achieve stability and security, it must give the policy of social justice higher priority than industrialization. In most Asian nations, the end and means have been turned upside-down, with the policy of industrialization placed far above the priority of social justice. This is exactly the opposite of what Matthew 6:33 tells us. Probably many Asian policy-makers sincerely believe in giving the first priority of national policy-options to industrialization since without economic affluence no policy of social welfare can be feasible.

But my strong contention is that industrialization can at best be a means to an end, and never be an end in itself. The ultimate aim of industrialization is the welfare of people. This being so, the exploitation of people is putting the cart before the horse. If the sacrifice of today's generation to the god of industrialization is the only way to accomplish modernization, then Mao's China, especially during the era of the Great Leap Forward in the late 1950s, is the best model for all other Asian nations to follow. All the means of mass exploitation, along with forced labor camps and the secret police, can well be justified in the sacred name of industrialization.

Even apart from moral considerations, I have two practical reasons for disagreeing with the present economic policies of Asian governments. First, to push industrialization by letting workers live on slave wages kills their incentive. Labor organizations do exist, but in name only, because the "labor aristocrats" allied with the political power elite help capitalists exploit the workers. Naturally, labor efficiency diminishes, thereby decelerating the speed of in-dustrialization.

Second, the promise of the welfare state has proven to be illusory. Ever since the Meiji Restoration of 1868, Japan, for instance, has carried out industrialization largely with the capital accumulated through the exploitation of the farmers and workers; but the outcome of this effort in the prewar era was the birth of the military (Kumbatsu) state. In the postwar era, although she ranks third among the industrial nations, the dream of a welfare state in Japan is as remote as ever.

Instead of moving toward a welfare state, Japan has be-come a corporate oligopoly dominated largely by a few major *zaibátsu* and *konzerns*. This case demonstrates that industrialization does not automatically bring affluence and welfare to the downtrodden masses. What troubles most Asian countries today is not so much the production of material goods as the distribution of its fruits.

To give political rights to people existing on a subhuman level means little. Man's basic desire for survival must be met before he can value other freedoms. The freedom from want must not be dealt with as a subsidiary question com-ing in order of importance after political freedom, for all the freedoms that we value are organically bound together.

Now we have arrived at a new field of study, the field of economics. What is the best available economic order that we as Christians must strive to support? What is the best road to material plentitude which the Bible endorses?

2. BEYOND CAPITALISM AND SOCIALISM

Living as we do in indigence and seeing the suffering of people in need about us, no sensible Christian thinker in Asia can regard economic progress as devilish and detri-mental to spiritual growth. On the contrary, we the Asian Christians are as much committed to economic moderniza-tion as any non-Christian, or even more so, for the task of salvation must be to save the whole man, not just a part of man.

But beyond this point, no concensus exists. Hopelessly divided among many conflicting economic schools of thought and confounded by the ever-increasing rate of economic change in recent times, Asian Christian leaders have no commonly acceptable business ethics or economic doctrines. With logical and well-organized arguments, some support private property rights as inviolably sacred; and with equally convincing points others condemn such rights as direfully diabolic. Some think the capitalistic system is an outgrowth of biblical doctrines, while others side with socialism and maintain economic egalitarianism as the ideology that is essentially biblical.

However, the Bible concentrates on man's salvation and not economic thought, so it provides us with little specific teaching that could be applicable to the current situation in Asia. Yet I believe that the Word of God provides some basic guidelines, and Christian beliefs, if put into practice, can exert a decisive influence upon the economic system of every society.

Max Weber stands out among those Western ideologues who have delved into this challenging subject. Seeing that since time immemorial the rich have had egoistic motives, but that no human civilization except the West has succeeded in creating industrial capitalism, Weber discovered in Christian ethics—notably the Calvinistic beliefs of stewardship, asceticism, predestination, and calling—the link between religion and capitalism.

Despite the severe criticism directed at the Weberian thesis and the serious modifications of the thesis by R. H. Tawney and others, no one can underestimate the overwhelming influence of the Reformation upon the birth of modern economic systems. The Puritans of England, especially those who migrated to America, tried to mold their economic life in accordance with God's commandments, thereby giving birth to the capitalistic mode of economy.

John Wesley in the eighteenth century unintentionally justified capitalism, for his Methodist followers—by leading lives of diligence, honesty, and frugality—found that they became richer. After observing the inextricable linkage between pious religious life and economic affluence, Wesley defended wealth by saying that though prosperity might tempt faithful believers to sin, Christians could grow in grace by giving generously to the poor.[1] History has shown that an economic structure, whatever the form it might take, cannot stand without the support of noneconomic factors like ethical doctrines.

However, a serious reservation must be made at this point. Plausible as it may sound, the Weberian thesis must not be accepted in toto. Our endorsement of Weber's thought should not be construed as an unqualified and unequivocable support of capitalism. The identification of Christianity with any one socioeconomic system can be misleading. It may well be true that Christianity influenced the birth of industrial capitalism just as it exerted an influence upon the gestation of political democracy in the West, but the connection must not be unduly stretched beyond this point. The historical background of the interaction between Protestantism and capitalism can in no way be interpreted to mean that the capitalistic system is the offspring of Christianity.

Modern capitalism as seen today seems to recognize no value higher than immediate material gain, and by so doing has become anathema to Christianity. As Purnell H. Benson observes in his *Religion in Contemporary Culture*, "For the most part religious light has gone out of capitalism."[2] In the business world of our age, mutual trust and honesty do not exist as virtues. The dog-eat-dog struggle described in Darwin's law of the survival of the fittest goes on perpetually, so intensely that the Kingdom of God cannot be allied with today's capitalism.

If the capitalist system has become increasingly defunct in Western societies which had once been firmly grounded on Christian ethics, what more can we expect of its success in Asian societies which have no such ethical codes or moral power? I find that most Asian businessmen, without the Christian awareness of the sinfulness of human nature, seem to regard capitalism as a doctrine of selfishness—an economic doctrine which unleashes the desire for unlimited materialistic gain and justifies unethical business practices. With no moral force sustaining the capitalist system, laissez-faire policies in most non-Communist Asian countries have caused innumerable harmful effects.

At this juncture, dismayed by the dysfunction of the capitalist system, many Christian intellectuals have turned to socialism in their search for an alternative choice. This is an economic system which seems to have strong humanistic ideals and humanitarian strains. Echoing Christian socialism of the West which has turned against capitalistic exploitation, inequality, and free market philosophy, numerous socially conscious Christians in Asia have embraced socialism and strive to realize a system of public ownership and management of the means of production in their respective societies. In postwar Japan, for instance, Kagawa Toyohiko—a leading Christian thinker whose ideals were similar to those of Reinhold Niebuhr—became a founding member of the Japanese Socialist Party. In 1947, when the first socialist cabinet was born in Tokyo, Premier Katayama Tetsu was a Christian.

Today, however, we see that the socialist economic system is in no way superior to capitalism. No longer is socialism a fresh ideology untested in the Asian milieu. To our disappointment, we find furthermore that socialism breeds problems no less serious than those produced by the capitalist system.

With man's basic nature remaining unchanged, socialistic or communal ownership of property does not work, simply because people do not take care of public property as diligently as they do their own. The socialist system presently existing in many Asian countries such as Burma must eventually institutionalize terror, both physical and psychological, no less inhumane than that of the Soviet Union, if the socialist ownership of property is to be productive. A planned economy with public ownership of major industries and land is, in the expression of Friedrich Hayek, *The Road to Serfdom*. Despite their apparent differences, capitalism and socialism share striking similarities. Both are essentially anthropocentric and believe in the cult of Progress. Capitalism holds that man is basically self-centered, but entertains the naive hope, in line with the Enlightenment tradition, that the law of historical progress is the work of an "invisible hand." On the other hand, socialism is even more naive in believing that man is basically so benevolent that he will share material goods communally. Socialists simplistically see the possibility of a man-made utopia on earth by transforming social institutions in accordance with certain blueprints. Both ideologies have not, therefore, proven to be effective in meeting the problems of today's Asia.

Confronted by innumerable problems, unexpected and unresolvable, the Asian states which have adopted either capitalism or socialism are now becoming eclectic by combining elements of socialism, capitalism, and traditionalism, all at the same time, in their economic planning. Traditional communal ownership of public land, for example, wears new socialistic clothes without changing its substance. In the name of socialistic enterprises, the government takes the initiative in constructing industrial plants and in managing major transportation networks, but tries to leave private initiative in many sectors of the national economy.

In the end, however, what becomes increasingly evident is that an eclectic economy, instead of resolving problems, creates more serious ones. Insofar as there can be no clear line of demarcation between private ownership and public ownership and between government control and private initiative in the national economy, all the economic policies of a nation fall into the pit of improvisation and change from year to year or even from day to day.

Moreover, when the economic structure begins to fall apart, bureaucratic controls on the economic life of people are strengthened. Then the bureaucratization of the national economy produces gross waste and undesirable side effects. In such an eclectic system, government officials enrich themselves illegally. The socialist system in most Asian countries, as we see in Burma for example, has become virtually defunct.

I believe that neither the capitalist system nor the socialist system can claim to be perfect. Neither they nor any eclectic system can be free from corruption and subsequent disintegration. No matter how well lubricated the economic mechanism created from any ideological blueprint and no matter what the noble aims going along with it, contradictions in our society cannot be rooted out. Good and evil coexist in every economic system.

Is there then no economic system which can be identified with Christianity? If not, should Christians devise a blueprint? To both questions, the biblical answer is no. I do not find any justification for identifying the Christian church with the latifundium of the Romans or the feudal system of Medieval Europe. In the same vein, it is grossly erroneous to equate Puritanism with the American capitalistic system of today. To regard an economic system as sacrosanctly inviolable is, in effect, idolatrous and unbiblical, for social systems, structures, and institutions are always untenable and are constantly being remolded in the flux of historical time. Christian realism, refusing to sanctify any socioeconomic system, reminds us of shortcomings existing in every society and spurs us to reform institutionalized sins in every economic structure.

But the Bible is, paradoxically enough, ahistorical and historical, both at the same time. Biblical teachings transcend human history, and by shedding spiritual light upon our path show clearly what common goals every human society should strive to realize. Although the Word of God does not provide us with elaborate organizational blueprints, it lays a vital spiritual foundation for our economic life.

I find that the biblical teachings which can be extrapolated for economic questions are implied in its theocentric *Weltanschauung*, a world-view strictly based upon the acceptance of the sovereignty of God over all existence, both material and spiritual.

Whereas the Oriental religions such as Hinduism and Buddhism unduly accentuated the negation of man's physical life for the sake of his spiritual salvation, Christianity, believing the material world to be God's creation, tried to balance man's life between the spiritual world and the physical world. That being the case, Christians cannot regard matter as something inherently evil. Without a mind of its own—a mind which can judge good from evil—matter is neutral, neither good nor evil. Only man's mind, if it places material value above everything else, can make material possession diabolic.

However, the Bible goes deeper than this. A fact which we must constantly bear in mind is that God did not give us the title to material possessions. God did not tell Adam and Eve that they could conquer, plunder, and destroy natural resources at will. In Genesis 1:28, God said to them: "Be fruitful, and multiply, and replenish the earth, and subdue it; and have dominion over the fish of the sea, and over the fowl of the air, and over every living thing that moveth upon the earth." In effect, Adam and Eve were told that they did not own the Garden of Eden; it was merely entrusted to them to manage for the glory of God.

Time and time again, the Bible reiterates the sovereignty of God over all things on earth. Exodus 19:5 says, "all the earth is mine." Here, at this point, Christian economic thought transcends both capitalism and socialism. Man cannot own property either individually (capitalistic) or collectively (socialistic), for everything existing in the world, including man himself, belongs to God. Nothing can exist outside of the realm of His grace. Everything depends upon Him for existence. God is the sole owner of nature, man, and history. This sounds extremely unpractical, too abstract to be acceptable to the modern mind, but history demonstrates that this biblical idea about property ownership has proven itself to be the most practical, pragmatic, and productive doctrine for economic development.

By admitting God's ownership of material goods and by negating man's property ownership, individually and collectively, man normalizes his relationship with nature. What terrible crimes are committed against nature these days because of man's misconception of his ownership! Man has no right to destroy nature, to exhaust natural resources, and to pollute the air and water in the name of economic progress. This kind of progress, if left unchecked, will eventually drive him into the abyss of self-annihilation. The bio-ecological environment of our world has become dangerously deranged and unbalanced. By sacrificing nature on the altar of unchecked economic development, man has recklessly destroyed his own biosphere. How can we stop this ecocidal trend?

Cassandras are not lacking. Movements for the conservation of nature spring up in the West and in the East but the overall situation has not improved. With every Asian nation working towards industrialization at unprecedented speed, the problem of pollution has been aggravated.

In my opinion, this problem cannot be rectified unless and until man renounces the erroneous belief that he owns nature. Anthropocentrism is self-defeating and self-destructive. It blinds man and leads him to destruction. Therefore, the belief in God's ownership is more than a mere religious decision. By surrendering everything we have to Him, we can gain the real foundation for enjoying all things in the world.

By admitting God's ownership of the material world, we can channel the power of science-technology in a more constructive direction, instead of driving the world to the brink of Armageddon. The present relation of man and science-technology has reversed the proper order. Science-technology supposedly exists for man. Through it, he can understand the hidden forces of nature and make use of them for his betterment; but with science-technology moving by its own laws independent of human will, man is no longer the master of his own destiny. How can we reverse this inverted relationship?

Many humanists think that science-technology is inherently evil and suggest ways and means to turn it to the service of man, instead of allowing man to continue to serve it. They talk about the innate danger of the mega-machine and the need for taming it. Nevertheless, their arguments miss the point. Science-technology has no independent will of its own. The real culprit is, ironically enough, none other than man himself. Here again is a typical example of the law of paradox working in history, for man's efforts to fulfill his desires through science-technology have created a Frankenstein. On the other hand, if man earnestly seeks God's Kingdom by utilizing the power of science-technology, he can be assured of great happiness, both spiritually and materially.

By admitting God's ownership of the material world, we can answer the outcry of the downtrodden peoples throughout Asia and pave the way for social justice, without which no society can be stabilized.

In today's Asia, the distribution of wealth poses a problem directly linked to economic productivity. The industrialization of most Asian nations, both Communist and non-Communist, is being carried out with the capital accumulated through relentless exploitation of the laboring masses. This method has reached marginal efficiency. The Gross National Product goes up almost every year, but in sharp contrast the life of the average man remains the same, or proportionately worsens. Political leaders, perhaps with an ounce of good intention, try to persuade the rich to share more of their wealth with the poor, but no amount of persuasion can impel the rich to do so. Inexorably, economic power and political power are intertwined. If this disparity continues, many Asian nations may veer toward violent revolution.

The Communist revolutions destroyed the rich with brutal violence, only to install a new ruling class as ruthless in exploiting the masses as was the old power elite. In Asian Communist countries, collectivization of farm lands has been carried out far more thoroughly and ruthlessly than it was during the Stalin era of the Soviet Union. Apart from changing their status from that of a landless tenant to that of a working tool of the collective farm, the average peasant of the Communist nations has gained little. Living conditions among industrial workers are no better. Regimented into militaristic industrial organizations for forced labor and deprived of all human rights, they are being robotized and mechanized. Dehumanization characterizes all Communist societies.

With this reality, I believe that no amount of revolutionary upheaval can realize a just and righteous society in which exploitation will disappear. Institutional changes are often necessary, but they cannot automatically bring social justice or ameliorate the social ills vexing us today. I think that we can ease, if not solve, the problems of social injustice only by instilling the biblical concept of property ownership into the minds of those who hold the power. People will be treated as human beings only when they are regarded as the children of God. Only with an awareness of the Lordship of God over the material world may the underprivileged masses claim their inalienable rights for freedom from want, and may the privileged rich learn to share their wealth with those who are in need.

In no sense do I, however, imply that wealth is evil and that money is the source of all evils. Nothing is further from the truth. Although the Bible says that "a rich man shall hardly enter into the kingdom of heaven" (Matthew 19:23),

Christianity does not condemn wealth *per se*. The question of good and evil lies in man's mind—the mind which makes decisions about how material goods are to be used. If used for good works, money can bring forth many blessings for man's welfare. The Bible, therefore, acknowledges this important fact in that it praises the good works of such rich men as Abraham, Job, and Joseph of Arimathaea. Deuteronomy 8:18 says that wealth is a gift of God, for God "giveth thee power to get wealth." In this sense, I believe that Christians should have more, and better, reasons to earn money insofar as God's work on earth needs money.

Christian stewardship of material goods requires accountability, however. In the parable of the nobleman who left home for a journey "to receive for himself a kingdom," Christ told His disciples:

> And he called his ten servants, and delivered them ten pounds, and said unto them, Occupy till I come. . . . And it came to pass, that when he was returned, having received the kingdom, then he commanded these servants to be called unto him, to whom he had given the money, that he might know how much every man had gained by trading (Luke 19:12-15).

Christians who manage God's property must be aware of this responsibility to increase wealth and be willing to give generously to the cause of His Kingdom whenever they are so demanded. To give one tenth of our earnings to God is, therefore, not enough, but many of us rob God even "in tithes and offerings" (Malachi 3:8).

To a greater or lesser degree, all of us rob God in one way or another. We tend to put more faith in our wealth than in Christ. Christian realism consequently warns the rich in wealth and in spirit, pointing out the fact that "love of money is the root of all evil" (1 Timothy 6:10). Psalm 62:10 says, "If riches increase, set not your heart upon them." In the same vein, if a society's material gain is the only collec-

tive goal it seeks, materialism resulting from this one-
dimensional life of people will eventually lead it to destruction. If, on the contrary, a society seeks, "first the kingdom
of God, . . . all these things shall be added" unto it (Matthew 6:33).

This theocentric concept of material possession can be the
spiritual foundation of business ethics on which an economic system may productively operate. I believe that so
long as this cardinal teaching of the Bible is respected, it
matters little what economic institutions a society adopts.
This doctrine, unworldly as it may sound, can make society
materially prosperous and economically wholesome, sane,
and stable. The evangelization of people, therefore, is more
than a mere spiritual upheaval. It should have a deep socioeconomic impact upon the life of a society, for it creates a
spiritual milieu. Slow as it is, this is the best biblical
method for restoring man's normal relation with the material world, paving the way for economic progress.

"For by their fruits you shall know them." This biblical
injunction can also be used to judge between a sane economic system and an insane one. If the fruits of production
go to a small group of people, either to individuals as in
capitalistic society or collectively to the power elite as in
socialistic society, we Christians cannot support such a
structure. If, in the name of God, an economic system gears
itself to establishing an egalitarian society even if such can
not be completely realized in human history, we can support it. This seemingly simplistic yardstick of judgment
suggests a few points for further deliberation.

First, a sane economic system must base itself upon
Christian realism, the kind of realism which sees man's
potential to be good and bad at the same time. In the economic realm, man is prone to act on the basis of his own
selfish interests. This being the case any economic system
denying or ignoring this brutal reality cannot endure for
long. Because of this realism, Christianity recognizes private property as a basis of the economic structure. We do

so, not because it is the best basis of an economic system, but because it is the lesser of many evils in historical reality.

If there is no possibility of possessing something tangible, man simply refuses to work. The selfish tendency of human nature must be accepted as an immutable fact of economic life. The Communist economic system which naively negates profit as a major motivating force for economic activities finds itself compelled to make people work by means of institutionalized terrorism. Man works hard without being compelled to do so by authority so long as he knows he can enrich himself in the process. Competition spurs him to drive himself. The economic progress of society results from this competitive mechanism working among the people.

There is another reason to support this position. While working to earn something for himself or for his family, man expresses himself freely, fulfilling his innate talents— the individual talents that God has given to each one of us. Freedom is essential if a man is to fulfill his potential when he engages in work. In this sense, Christianity sees Communism as an ideology too idealistic to be really practical. By refusing to see man as he is, Communism treats him as something other than human.

But this recognition of private property does not imply that man has a limitless right to amass fortunes and dispose of his possessions at will. In Christian economic thought everything existing in the universe ultimately belongs to God, and all man does is to manage what God temporarily has entrusted to him. Just as in the parable of the servant entrusted with five talents, we have to increase our wealth for God's glory in meekness and regard wealth as a means to an end, but not an end in itself.

On innumerable occasions, Christ admonished us not to make the increasing of wealth our goal in life, and made it abundantly clear that one of the best ways to serve God with our wealth is to give to the poor. Therefore, serving God is not something abstract. It is as concrete as the existence of needy people in our society. To give to the poor is not, as many Christians believe, an act of philanthropy. It is, on the contrary, paying God what is due to God (Luke 20:25). We should, without grudging, return our possessions to God whenever they are so demanded.

Second, there is, however, only a slight possibility of man's accepting this moral and ethical standard. Since most societies, made up as they are of sinners, cannot be completely evangelized, there must be some institutional safeguards to limit the power of the rich and to protect the poor from being exploited.

With its increasingly complex roles in the wake of rapid social change, modern government is vested with the responsibility of guarding the right of the economically downtrodden to enjoy at least a basic subsistence level of living. Through various methods of taxation, income redistribution, and social welfare, the government is expected to protect the poor from being "ground up" by the rich (Isaiah 3:15). But as noted previously, the present conditions in most Asian countries fall short of this goal, especially in view of the fact that so often political power exists only for the privileged classes. As Christians, we must be aware of this brutal reality. Individually and collectively we should strive to foster a political milieu in which the government may serve the "have-nots" instead of rendering itself a tool of "the haves."

In this pathetic situation, perhaps the best available safety device for the laboring class is organizing themselves into various interest or pressure groups, such as labor unions or peasant unions. In this age of big business no single individual dare say anything against gigantic corporations. Working people must obtain their fair share by bargaining for their demands collectively. However, here again, the present situation in Asia is gloomy. No Asian society has so far allowed or endeavored to foster a free atmosphere for the toiling masses to develop unions sufficiently strong to cope with powerful business interests allied with the political power.

A warning, however, seems imperative here. To side with the poor does not in any sense mean that Christians should instigate a class war in every society the way Marxism suggests. Christian realism tells us that sin is pervasive in all people irrespective of social class. Frederick Catherwood writes that "the rich are sinners, but so are the poor."[3] To condemn one social class for the selfish interests of another social class is not a Christian method. As Christians, we think of the interests of the poor mainly because they, being so deprived and impoverished, need our love, and certainly not because of our blind hatred of the wealthy class. The Kingdom of God transcends all social classes and aims at achieving an egalitarian society—a society of love and cooperation, not of class enmity and strife.

In conclusion, I believe that we Asian Christians can spur economic progress by instilling biblical teaching into the economic life of our people. It may be a slow, tedious process, but it is the surest way to bring forth material affluence. A sound economic system is one which at least tries to reflect the image of the Kingdom of God in all areas of its activities. In brief, an economic system must be theocentric if, paradoxically enough, it wants to serve man.

As Christians, therefore, we must be prudent about naive utopian schemes like Communism and socialism. Our belief in God's Kingdom as our ultimate goal makes us practical in our everyday lives and truly pragmatic in choosing the least of many evils, instead of looking for the man-made blueprints of any one economic system. To make any one economic structure sane and wholesome requires an unceasing struggle on our part, for after all, any economic institution or structure existing in historical time is the creation of sinful man. Only by putting our goal in the Kingdom of God, the perfect realm ruled by God, can we reform, regenerate, and recast our economic system, and better our life and achieve social progress, all at the same time.

3. BEYOND NATIONALISM AND COSMOPOLITANISM

When we turn our attention to world affairs, we become more confused. So many diversified and multifarious metamorphoses take place in our world at such phenomenal speed that we can hardly describe the overall historical condition of our age in intelligible, comprehensive terms. Our world is characterized by ambivalence—ambivalence in the sense that both centripetal and centrifugal forces are at work simultaneously, unifying and separating peoples at the same time.

On one hand, the world has become a single, indivisible living space for mankind. Peoples of different ethnic and cultural origins who had no contact in the past have come to know each other quite intimately. The world is reduced to a "global village" with nations increasingly interdependent. This situation, more than anything else, has given rise to pan-mankind consciousness which, if developed continuously in a genial atmosphere, may well become a new spiritual foundation for world peace.

But on the other hand we see centrifugal forces break mankind into innumerable fragments and create inimical feelings among different peoples with an intensity never seen before. As physical contact among peoples of different social, cultural, and religious origins increases, the psychological gap between them widens instead of diminishes. Misunderstandings often break out into open hostilities and bloodshed. Instead of peace and harmony, anarchy and strife rule international affairs, and the threat of a holocaust hovers over all the world. Friction can ignite an Armageddon at any moment, at any place, and over any issue no matter how insignificant.

Our world is far from being the world of détente that impetuous journalists so often label it. Torn by misunderstandings among different peoples, confused by a series of blows like the dollar crisis and the oil crisis, and unable to find a new direction in which to move, our world stands helplessly at the brink of total annihilation. In international affairs every nation has become increasingly selfish. Even in American foreign policy, the Wilsonian type of moral diplomacy has long since ceased to exist. Why should the United States be its "brother's keeper" indefinitely? Great Britain, dwindling into a little England, acts more and more on its national interests alone, and France sells lethal arms to any nation, so long as such deals are lucrative. Neo-nationalism is rising high.

In Asia, after the so-called Nixon shock, most nations are bent on seeking nothing but their national self-interests. Fearful of becoming pawns of the present détente among the great powers, the smaller Asian nations hide under the turtle shell of nationalism as a means of survival. Suspicious of the international anarchy which recognizes no rule but "might is right," and fearful of the secret deals of power politics made by the big powers, most Asian nations have found no other course for survival except by pursuing their own national interests.

As Sir Frederick Catherwood points out, "nationalism is the religion" of many Asian nations and is more potent and powerful than Marxism, "because it is a religion of the heart and not of the head."[4] Even in Red China, North Korea, and North Vietnam, nationalism has gained momentum to such an extent that Communism has become nationalistic. The end of ideology in Asia proves to be the new age of nationalism. It is a new sacred cow to which all other values are readily sacrificed.

As Christians, what must be our proper attitude toward nationalism?

In the West, Christian thinkers are generally, if not totally, against nationalism and regard it as something antithetical to the Gospel. The memories of Fascism and Nazism are still fresh in their minds. Especially in the present time, nationalism has become identified with the sectionalism of the Scots, the Welsh, the Basques, the Flemish, and the Walloons. Witnessing this historical reality, they

see that the Bible, a universal message to every people irrespective of their race or color, is in sharp disagreement with
the basic tenets of nationalism. Sir Frederick Catherwood
says: "If ever there was a case for nationalism, surely it was
the case of God's chosen people. Yet Jesus turned His back
on that case. He was not interested in Jewish nationalism."[5]
Should we Asian Christians be in full agreement with this
judgment?

In history we are reminded that during the era immediately before World War II, Western missionaries, particularly in Southeast Asia, took a strong stand, not without
some convincing reasons, against nationalism; but we
know that their unswerving antinationalist stance unwittingly served the interests of Western colonialists by alienat-
ing native Christians from national independence movements. Asian Christians were given the stigma of pro-
colonialism which still remains.

Only in Korea was the situation different. Inasmuch as
Korea was under Japanese colonial rule, Western missionaries identified themselves with Korean nationalism
not by instigating anti-Japanese xenophobia among the
people, but by instilling in them the idea that freedom,
individual or national, was a God-given gift which should
be regained. For the Koreans, the best possible way to regain freedom, including that of religious worship, was to
engage in struggles for national liberation from the
Japanese yoke, and the Korean church supported
nationalist movements in every possible way. Therefore as
Christians we must not be hasty in condemning
nationalism. Everything existing in history usually has two
sides, the aspect of good and that of evil, and nationalism is
no exception.

If we speak purely in secular terms, nationalism is a feeling of solidarity which binds a large group of people in the
belief of a common destiny. Some scholars think of "blood
ties" as the basis of nationalism; but since there is no such
thing as unmitigated and pure racial or ethnic blood, this

theory is at best a myth with little historical validity, and yet a myth which, if translated into political action as seen in the case of Nazism, can be virulent.

Another group of scholars maintain that nationalism is a product of the love of people for the land in which they live, the land which gives them common experiences of joy and misery in life. But this theory, plausible as it appears, cannot be entirely valid in view of the fact that the Jews, for instance, maintained a strong nationalism for millenia without any common territorial possession. Still others insist that nationalism is the product of the common culture that a group of people share, for this cultural milieu makes them think, feel, act, and behave in the same way. But this theory too is vulnerable to criticism because the Spanish culture, for example, could not unite all the South American peoples in a common nationalism.

As a historian, I view nationalism as a historical product in the sense that it, unlike the things of natural genesis, comes to exist in time as a human psychic response to particular historical conditioning. Similar to tribalism, but much greater in scale, nationalism is gradually, or sometimes suddenly, generated in the minds of people who after a long period of experiencing historical events together think of themselves as bound by a common destiny. In the ancient world, nationalistic feelings were not entirely absent, but they were overshadowed by tribalism, kingdomism, and empire-building and thus could not grow into the common, comprehensive ideology we know today.

In the history of Western civilization, for instance, we see no nationalism in the early Middle Ages. In that particular stage of historical development in the West, tribalism and universalism were juxtaposed in a strange mixture known as feudalism. The ideal of empire—a historical heritage from the Romans was resuscitated in the Carolingian Empire and in the Holy Roman Empire, but it existed only in the imagination of people, for the society was completely feudalized.

But by the time of the High Middle Ages, with the rise of new historical forces such as the middle class and the new monarchy, movements to unify feudal domains into a number of nation-states gained momentum; and the intellectual revolution, the economic revolution, and the scientific revolution of the period, together with the phenomenal development of weaponry, spurred the rise of nation-states, with nationalism serving as their founding ideology. The breakdown of the universal church into many rival denominations also stepped up the growth of nationalism.

Among the modern nation-states, England was the first nation which perfected aspirations of nationalism. By the sixteenth century, she had a well-developed national language, a middle class, a national church, and a viable institution of the monarchy—the four indispensable elements of modern nationalism. Compared with England, the national unification of Germany and Italy came much later.

Being historical, not natural, nationalism may disappear in historical time. What I mean to say is that it is not something that must stay with mankind forever. If and when history reaches a higher plane of development in which the nation-state can no longer serve as the political unit, there will be a time when nationalism may well become a vestige of history just as tribalism is in the advanced societies today. It is highly conceivable that someday human beings may find another basis of solidarity, a new ideology much bigger and stronger than nationalism.

Today, in the late twentieth century, we see regionalism in Europe rising, adamantly and steadfastly, as though it is ready to replace nationalism. Of course, Europe is still far from being one unit despite the establishment of the Steel and Coal Community and subsequently the European Economic Community (E.E.C.). The dream of one Europe thrives in spite of hazardous dangers as was so well demonstrated by the movement in Britain to pull out from the nine-nation E.E.C. To the dismay of many European idealists who hope to realize a United States of Europe in their lifetime, sectional rifts in every European society have become manifest. Yet with all the wranglings and disputes, we can see that the progress of Western European integration moves on, making breakthroughs which up until recently seemed well-nigh impossible.

First, the traditional hostilities among the European nations, notably between Germany and France, have been considerably eased, if not completely eradicated, with no prospect of another total war among them. Second, a great portion of each nation's sovereign power has been transferred to regional policy-making bodies such as the Euratom. Third, political transnationality has become plainly apparent in the works of social organizations such as the labor union. Fourth, people can travel to other countries as though all of Western Europe were one political unit. Donald Puchala observes that "national identifications have not altered very much, but in increasing fashion, they have been supplemented by regional identification."

Will regional identification eventually replace national identification? The answer is anybody's guess. At present such a prospect appears dim, almost impossible. But at the same time, we see that regionalism looms large in the Middle East in the form of the Arab League; and to a much lesser extent, it is growing in Africa and in Latin America. Only in Asia, for various reasons, do we find that regionalism is not increasing.

Along with regionalism, the newly rising cosmopolitanism calls for a Christian appraisal. In these days when the world is so hopelessly torn by political ideologies, racism, and nationalism, it becomes increasingly imperative for us to think in terms of cosmopolitanism. No nation can be an island; every people belongs to a universal brotherhood.

Already some clamor for the establishment of a world government as the best way for mankind to avoid an Armageddon. The maximalists propose to organize a strong, centralized form of government which, soaring beyond and above nationalism, could absorb the sovereignty of the existing nation-states, while the minimalists want to establish a decentralized, federated form of government. Opinions are varied on how to set up such a world government. Garry Davis, for instance, advocates the idea of "a peaceful conspiracy" with schemes to overthrow all the existing governments as a means to establishing it. David Mitrany, on the other hand, finds hope in a functional approach by which nonpolitical organizations, such as the labor unions, of each nation could functionally integrate their activities on a global scale. Inasmuch as none of these suggestions are, at this stage, taken seriously by most of the political leaders in today's world, the idea of establishing a world government remains in a raw, crude form, with no realistic plans to implement it.

All in all, we find here again that we live in a great transitional period in which the elements of both the past and the present are mixed. We find that as on the physical plane people in different parts of the world have increasingly closer and more frequent contact, on the psychic plane the differences among them become more distinct. Hence, a man may talk like a cosmopolitan, but act like a chauvinist. Or a man may work for regionalism, but at heart be a racist.

Conversely we find that people cannot be strictly classified into these three categories. A man who really loves his nation can at the same time work for the cause of universal brotherhood. Ideals of regionalism can be useful for international cooperation. What I mean to say here is that these ideologies, despite popular misconceptions to the contrary, are not mutually exclusive and antagonistic. By accepting one of them and negating the others, one may become a bigot.

At this point, speaking of a Christian attitude toward these ideologies, I find a generally accepted misconception among most Christians of Asia. In many Asian Christian circles, nationalism is regarded as something antithetical to the Gospel while cosmopolitanism is taken as something biblical.

Of course there is little doubt that Christianity has been ecumenical from the very beginning. God created Adam and Eve, the parents of all mankind, and in Him there cannot exist any difference between the Jews and the Greeks and by the same token between the Chinese and the Americans. But Christian realism goes deeper than this idealism, deeper into the reality of human history. The Bible, the greatest single source of idealism, is simultaneously a book of realism. As Christians, we must therefore see every historical question squarely, both idealistically and realistically.

After the fall of man, the ideal of universal brotherhood among men persisted in the human psyche, but it could not materialize in historical time as a reality. The major reason for this pathetic situation, according to Christian realism, is the sinful nature of man. Cain killed his own brother, Abel, for no reason other than jealousy. Since the Deluge, as the population on earth grew by leaps and bounds and spread to many continents, there existed no sociopolitical matrix in which cosmopolitanism could germinate. In primitive life which could have no elaborate systems of communication and transportation, the most practical ways of uniting peoples in each locality were tribalism and clanism.

Christian realism tells us that God, the Lord of human history, provides man with sociopolitical organizations suitable to each particular historical situation. The tribal structure was both necessary and practical in the period of pre-civilization, but with the progress of human culture man was given a new, larger unit of sociopolitical organization known today as "nation." God permitted nations to rise up, and on some occasions specifically created them to serve His eternal plans in human history.

Speaking to Abraham about leaving the land of his fathers, God said: "I will make of thee a great nation" (Genesis 12:2). Later, when the Israelites were mistreated by the Egyptians, God told Moses to talk to them: "I will bring you up out of the affliction of Egypt, unto the land of the Canaanites, and the Hittites, and the Amorites, and the Perizzites, and the Hivites, and the Jebusites, unto a land flowing with milk and honey" (Exodus 3:17). Here we see that the Jewish nation emerged in human history with God's blessings, to do his work as commanded.

In the Old Testament practically all the ancient Jewish prophets were patriots. They loved their people and were willing to die for them. When their people fell into sinning, they risked their lives to call them back to the righteous path of God. Isaiah 1:3 reads: "The ox knoweth his owner, and the ass, his master's crib, but Israel doth not know; my people doth not consider."

In the New Testament, our Lord was compassionate in seeing the miseries of his people and healed both their spiritual and physical wounds. Though called to the Gentiles, Paul was not without love of his own people. In Romans 9:1-3, Paul wrote: "I say the truth in Christ, I lie not, my conscience also bearing me witness in the Holy Ghost, that I have great heaviness and continual sorrow in my heart. For I could wish that I myself were accursed from Christ for my brethren, my kinsmen according to the flesh."

However, caution seems necessary at this point, in view of the fact that many people today confuse the love of one's nation with chauvinism. Christians love their nation as much as non-Christians, and in many respects even much more; but we do not place the nation on the very top of our value hierarchy while chauvinists, on the other hand, demand that people worship the nation with religious fervor. At times, as dual citizens of God's City and of our nation, we have to obey the higher laws of God when political leaders try to impose upon us the cult of nation. Often, all too often, we rebuke the sins of our nation. But eventually our obedience to God's laws makes our nation stronger and our country a better place in which to live. In contrast, chauvinism invariably leads a nation to total destruction.

Nor do we place cosmopolitanism on the very top of our

value hierarchy. Knowing the overall popular historical trend toward one world, Christians must partake in the movement of fostering a genial international milieu in the spirit of universal brotherhood, but this does not necessarily mean that the realization of one world is our supreme goal. Nothing could be further from our goal. Christ did not die on the cross for cosmopolitanism, nor for a world government.

I believe that our goal is the realization of the City of God in each nation, in each region, and ultimately in the whole world. The City of God is above and beyond nationalism, regionalism, and cosmopolitanism. It is far more precious than the world government for which many modern ideologues clamor. To the sophisticated minds of our age, this Christian goal of seeking God's Kingdom first, above all other values, may sound utterly unrealistic, but paradoxically history shows us overwhelming evidence that our efforts to realize God's City on earth will make our nation stable and regional cooperation and world government possible. Without believing in the Lordship of God over human destiny, how can we become genuinely altruistic in loving our compatriots or in loving other peoples of the world as our brothers and sisters?

4

Transfiguration of Asia

As seen in the previous chapter, the age of ideologies which has so conspicuously characterized the postwar era is about over. Amid the wrangles of ideological struggle between the United States and the Soviet Union, we Asians have tried hard to remodel our societies based on the patterns suggested by sociopolitical ideologies. However, standing in the second half of the 1970s, we find that these ideological blueprints are untenable, impracticable, and inapplicable. In the wake of the rapidly changing historical situation, they have become outmoded and outdated theories that if put into effect will create more complicated, unresolvable problems rather than giving solutions to many questions presently vesing us.

All the countries of today's Asia are now in a great transition. Living as we do in a time of rapidly accelerating historical change, we often view things solely in terms of change and tend to worship the cult of change, with little or no sense of direction. In brief, we are caught in a grand-scaled transmutation with no future goal. As a consequence, change creates more confusion. Old things are fast passing away, but no new daybreak has dawned. Where can we find new light? The only way to make historical progress is to change our spiritual milieu on the basis of God-centrism. God-centrism must permeate our life individually, socially, and culturally.

1. TRANSFIGURATION OF THE SPIRITUAL MILIEU

Liberal democracy, in its efforts to take root in the Asian

163

soul during the past three decades, has demonstrated its marginal utility. In Indonesia, in the Philippines, and in South Korea, the American form of liberal democracy could not adapt itself in the indigenous soils. In these countries, "the so-called democratic forms had become parodies of the ideal," or to put it differently, writes Carlos P. Romulo of the Philippines, "the undemocratic tendencies of the old society found it an unmitigated opportunity to assert themselves under the guise of democratic forms." In the 1970s, most non-Communist Asian countries took the form of "constitutional authoritarianism," according to Ferdinand E. Marcos, President of the Philippines. This is a new form of government which is unique in that "it does not seek to maintain the status quo but has instead brought about radical reforms."[1] The real viability of this new form of government has, however, not yet been proven clearly in historical time, and the political situation of these nations is still fluid.

Equally interesting is the decline of Communism as an ideology of social salvation. The dramatic fall of Indo-China into the hands of Communists in 1975 marked a decisive step in Communist expansion in Asia. The unified Vietnam, a nation of forty million people with an army that is one of the world's largest, poses a lethal threat to the rest of the Southeast Asian countries. Both Thailand and Malaysia are internally shaken by Communist guerrilla forces. Many Asian intellectuals are apprehensive of the possibility that all Asian countries might soon be drawn into the Communist camp.

But at the same time, it appears that Communism in Asia has lost its fresh appeal. The terrible, horrible, and outrageous stories leaking from Cambodia since the Communist Khmer Rouge's victory shocked us all. The sacrifice of human lives demanded by the Communists has been exorbitant. Over 600,000 Cambodians, roughly one-eighth of the nation's five million population, were reportedly massacred in the orgy of bloodbath. Nor do the reports coming out from Red China appeal to Asian minds. In the spring of 1976, angry mobs paying tribute to the late premier Chou En-lai went on a rampage in Peking in the worst outbreak of violence in China since the chaotic Cultural Revolution. More than 3,000 people, mostly young, were rounded up in the wake of the Tienanmen riots; and as Red China faces more serious troubles in connection with the succession question, Maoism may eventually dwindle into a totem of China's revolutionary past. Therefore, the Communist upsurge in Asia after the fall of Indo-China should not be interpreted as an irresistible, invincible wave but as something which could be broken and destroyed.

Nor can socialism show us the way to a brighter new future. Always ambiguous in principle and uncertain in its practical policies, socialism has no clear line dividing private ownership and the public control of economy and in the end creates more confusing problems. As the situation in Burma exemplifies, socialistic mechanisms have not proven to be as productive as commonly expected. Without strong ethical codes and moral power, a socialist system cannot take its roots in Asian soils. Creeping capitalism has become the order of the day in every socialistic system.

In this impasse, most Asian nations—especially these non-Communist nations—have become eclectic or "mixed" in adopting foreign ideological models. There now exists an economic continuum between capitalism and socialism and a political continuum extending from elite authoritarianism to mass democracy. However, these eclectic systems produce more and more confusion in our minds as well as in our societies.

On the basis of historical records, I can say in judgment that none of the "secular gospels"—liberal democracy, Communism, socialism, nationalism, syndicalism, authoritarianism, or totalitarianism—has been successful or viable enough to sustain our societies in perpetuity. I don't deny that in many parts of Asia these old ideologies are still strong in their influence upon social and intellectual change, but at the same time, it requires no scintillating acumen to see that we are standing on the threshold of a new era—the post-postwar era—which certainly lies beyond the age of ideologies.

In this deadlock, all kinds of humanism with high-sounding ideals have made headway into the Asian psyche. Many schools of humanism—anthropocentric ideals, atheistic and otherwise, upholding such concepts as human dignity and man's unlimited freedom—are in one accord in condemning the technology-dominated modern civilization which now characterizes the capitalist system, the socialist system, and the Communist system. Deploring the increasing alienation of man from what he has so elaborately and laboriously created in history, humanists advocate ideas to regain and reestablish humaneness and a humanitarian milieu in our life by urging every one of us to be humanitarian. But with all their high ideals, their influence has proven to be ephemeral. The law of paradox works here inversely. Without tackling the fundamental problem of modern civilization—the sinfulness of human nature—humanists tend to glorify their own humanitarian views and services, thereby falling into the pitfall of their own pride. Enlightened self-interest alone cannot make people truly altruistic or self-sacrificial.

On the other hand, we find that many Asian peoples are desperately trying to find a new breakthrough in the revival of their traditional heritages. But as previously discussed, these nostalgic movements cannot meet our expectations. As modernization makes headway in all realms of life, our spiritual heritage of the past will fast become outmoded and detrimental to progress.

Splendid as they were, the old traditions failed to goad social progress beyond the stage of agrarian life. How can they now direct our path to the future? If the past sheds light upon the present, we are reminded that the revival of our archaic heritages cannot rectify the problems arising from modernization. Looking into the past can be a necessary step for rediscovering our identity if we are not to be lost completely amid the tide of Western influence, but the nativistic reactions against Western civilization fall short of showing us a new direction in which to move.

Despite the many options presented to us we have, ironically enough, nothing to choose from. Sociopolitical ideologies that in the past claimed to be panaceas can no longer be considered sufficient to deal with the new problems confronting Asian societies. We find that the age of ideologies has gradually come to an end. There is a total deadlock from which no turning point or breakthrough is possible. All the anthropocentric ideologies and utopian schemes, increasingly diminishing in their influence, cannot meet our needs. Consequently, all of Asia is shrouded by an ominous cloud.

It is in this hopeless situation that we find the hope of Christianizing all the Asian peoples. At this dead end, the biblical teachings of the Kingdom of God shed new light upon our paths. To men of worldly wisdom having the Kingdom of God as our goal in life may appear foolhardy. But in this unworldly yet pragmatic principle lies the dynamics of God's Kingdom.

Christianity has been increasingly squeezed out in the West but it finds new and fertile ground in Asia. Despite the glorious traditional heritages of its past, Asia is in a gigantic spiritual interregnum, but unlike the West it has little anthropocentric self-complacency. With no achievements comparable to what the modern West has accomplished, we Asians do not have the superiority complex of Westerners. In this very humility lies the key to our future—a promising future for creating a new civilization based upon the spiritual dynamics of Christianity—the very foundation which the West has now forgotten.

My version of Christian optimism, cautious as it is, perhaps sounds highly unrealistic and is at best extremely vulnerable to criticism, for I cannot authenticate my claims with a convincing pile of empirical data. Numerically, the number of Christians in each Asian society, except in the Philippines, is still tiny; emotionally, Christianity has not yet shed the stigma of being a religion superimposed upon us by Western dominance. In practical terms the church is still seriously challenged by such reviving native spiritual traditions as Hinduism, Buddhism, Confucianism, and to a lesser degree Shintoism and Shamanism.

I am not blind to the reality that the total Christian population in Asia is very tiny, only 2 percent of the total 2.5 billion people. Statistically speaking, Christians constitute only 0.5 percent of the population in Thailand and Burma, 1 percent in Japan, 1.4 percent in Pakistan, 2.6 percent in Indonesia, 4 percent in Taiwan, 7.3 percent in Sri Lanka, 9 percent in Singapore, 12 percent in Korea, and 12 percent in Hong Kong. In the past, 13 percent of the Vietnamese and 1 percent of the Laotians and Cambodians were Christians, but since the Communist takeover of these nations, we do not know what has happened to them. Only in the Philippines do the majority of people, over 85 percent, profess to be Christians, but they do not seem to have strong evangelical zeal. To make things sound even more pathetic, Asian Christians are fragmented into petty sects and denominations. How can we then hope to see the evangelization of Asia within our generation?

Again, our hope can only be understood in paradoxical terms. Hope, as the story of Pandora's Box symbolizes, resides with despair. The hope of Christianization lies in the very fact of the hopelessness in today's Asia. The situation in Asia is critical, but the word "crisis" in Chinese is made of two words—danger and opportunity. Just as Christ started his ministry among the wretched people on the banks of the Galilee, we can shine the light of truth on the darkness in Asian minds. Since people cannot find any light in secular ideologies or in their traditional ideas they have become much more receptive to the Gospel.

During the colonial period, many Asian people refused to

accept Christ mainly because of the misconception that Christianity was a Western religion, a symbol of Western colonial domination. After passing through the trials and crises of the age of ideologies and witnessing the fatal shortcomings of the "secular gospels," many Asians now have changed their attitude toward Christianity. The fact that Jesus was born in Asia and His message was universal is generally, but quite clearly, understood now. With regard to preaching the Gospel, there has never been a more opportune time than today. In spite of all the present dangers, I still think that our age is the most exciting one to live in. We are in a time ripe for evangelization.

For instance, during the Korean War when the nation was in extreme danger, more Koreans accepted Christ than ever before. In Korea, I see that more young students are receptive to the Gospel today than at any time in the past. The rapid development of mass communication provides us with new opportunities for evangelization. At one single baptismal service, over 3,000 Korean soldiers were baptized. Despite the fact that Korea is not a Christian state, the system of chaplaincy has been a part of the proud tradition of the Korean Armed Forces. In 1975, when Billy Graham had an evangelistic crusade in Seoul, over one million Koreans packed a plaza to hear the Gospel. Never before had I seen so many people in one place. Never in the annals of Christian history did we see such a multitude coming to the Lord.

In Thailand, more and more Thais open their hearts to Christ. I was told that sales of the Bible tripled last year. The crisis in the country has created a new opportunity for God's Kingdom. Of late, in one two-year period over two and a half million Indonesians accepted Christ as their personal Savior. The same can be seen or expected in many other parts of Asia today. John Haggai, President of Haggai Institute, which trains Christian leaders in all walks of life, along with many other Christian thinkers, believes that "Asia and the South Pacific will be the great centers of

Christian activities and outreach during the coming decades."[2] What an exciting hope!

The uniqueness of Christianity has been proven, time
and time again, throughout the history of mankind. The
Gospel saves not only individual souls, but also societies
and civilizations from downfall. Faithful believers seeking
the Kingdom of God over and above all other desires of life
have spurred genuine social progress, while others seeking
to fulfill worldly desires have led society into destruction.
To devote one's life to the cause of His kingdom is therefore
not to lose worldly things. On the contrary it is the surest
way to gain all things on earth. The only hope we have in
today's Asia is evangelization. John Haggai writes:

> How can we hope? There is only one way—man's reconcili-
> ation to God and to each other through Jesus Christ. There is
> no shortcut, no easy way. Governments can't bring peace.
> Education can't bring it. Business and industry can't bring
> it. Psychology and sociology can't bring it. Only Christ can
> bring it.[3]

This is to say that our faith, our unswerving belief in
God, is the gestation of individual growth and social
progress. Without a firm belief in an omnipotent and om-
nipresent God, we cannot have strong convictions in making any serious decisions; and in the same vein, without
firm conviction in the Providence of God in human history,
we cannot take determined actions. Therefore, our faith in
God is the alpha and the omega of human history. In brief,
our spiritual milieu must be God-centric. By surrendering
to God all we possess—be it special talent or knowledge or
wealth—we can truly gain everything. If we are to change
the content of Rousseau's famous dictum, "return to nature," we can say that "returning to God" is the only way
for individual salvation and for the salvation of society. Let
us return to God. By turning to God, we can spur progress
in all realms of life. Christians become true revolutionaries
in that they perpetually reform their individual lives and

social institutions according to the divine light they receive from the Kingdom of God.

The return-to-God movement that I advocate stands against the naturecentrism of the East. As previously discussed, the old Oriental religions and philosophical schools of thought were essentially similar in that they were, without exception, naturecentric. Hindu gods were the personified forms in the forces of nature. In Hindu cosmology, all beings, physical and spiritual, existed in nature. Buddhism, an offspring of Hinduism, was fundamentally based upon naturecentrism. Every being in the universe had to obey, according to Buddhism, the immutable law of cause and effect, which in turn was tied to the eternal chain of cyclic time. Confucianism and Taoism in China derived their basic teachings from the ancient naturecentric cosmology—the theory of yin (negative) and yang (positive), the five elements theory, and the idea of ten heavenly stems and twelve earth branches. Granted that Confucianism had some strong strains of humanism, one can in no way deny that its humanistic elements were derivative of the naturecentric cosmology. Compared to these great religious and philosophical schools of thought, both Shamanism and Shintoism remained more crudely naturecentric.

Had our societies been chained to this naturecentrism indefinitely, Asian civilizations would not have been able to make scientific and technological leaps into the modern age. No decisive progress could have been possible.

At this point, I am not ignorant of the theory advanced by some Asian historians that the preindustrial stage of Asian civilizations could have produced modernity in due course of time even without the aid of Western culture. But I disagree. I am inclined to think that there is no law of inevitable progress in human history and that, this being the case, our ancient Eastern civilizations, so hopelessly trapped by naturecentric cosmological views, could not have jumped into the stage of industrialization without the modernizing influence of the West. Our premodern societies might have remained, by and large, in an agricultural stage almost indefinitely.

In the past the decline and fall of these powerful traditional Asian heritages was thought utterly inconceivable, too far-fetched and unimaginable to talk about. There was no Oswald Spengler in Asia, who boldly came out with a theory on the "decline" of old Asia. No force, social or intellectual, appeared to be strong enough to destroy, for instance, the tradition of Confucianism in China. A sharp decline of Shintoism in Japan was utterly unthinkable before World War II. It was simply impossible to speculate on the waning of Buddhism in Southeast Asia before the advent of the Western colonial powers. Nor was it possible to predict the decreasing influence of Hinduism in India, even after the establishment of the British colonial system in the country.

The coming of Western people to Asia began to change the scene, but colonial rule strengthened, rather than weakened, our old traditions. The revival of traditionalism was congenial with the rise of nationalism. It was, therefore during the postwar era that we began to see the erosion of traditional heritages in toto.

In China, it took no less a powerful force than Communism to smash, partially if not wholly, the heritages of Confucianism. In India, through the advancement of modern science and technology, the naturecentric cosmological views were somewhat weakened. Even the erstwhile powerful Islamic sects of Pakistan, Malaysia, and Indonesia have had to modify their basic tenets in the face of rapid industrialization and scientification. In Korea and in the Philippines, the Saemaul Movement (New Community Movement) and the New Society Movement, both initially directed by the respective governments, have succeeded in changing traditional modes of life and thought considerably.

Some may say that the residue of traditionalism is still

viable and, superficially at least, being resuscitated. Even highly educated Asians who in their daily life use scientific equipment and advanced technological devices do not seem to feel any contradiction when they visit fortune-tellers and go to worship their traditional gods in temples and shrines. In spite of his education in modern engineering, President Sukarno of Indonesia used to consult with astrologers almost as often as he sought the advice of economists. Even now, I hear many politicians in Asia consult with fortune-tellers before making their final decision about running for public office.

But with all these obvious facts, it may still be safe to predict that the naturecentric views of our traditionalism, unable to cope with the psychosomatic change brought forth by rapid modernization, will eventually fade away altogether. I sometimes feel that God is now using the secular gospels of man—the sociopolitical ideologies such as liberal democracy, Communism, socialism, anarchism, authoritarianism, and totalitarianism—to pave the way for the spread of the Gospel. Maoism in China, the other forms of Communism in North Korea, Vietnam, Laos and Cambodia, and the growing power of the government in other Asian nations are doing their mission—probably not God-given but God-permitted—to destroy the hard crusts and essential cores of our ancient traditions. Now the coming end of ideologies is opening a new chapter in the spread of Christianity throughout Asia.

However, at this point, what we must not overlook is the fact that Christian theocentrism does not destroy naturecentrism but instead, to the great surprise of nonbelievers, perfects it. In no way should we regard naturecentrism as something totally undesirable. Nor should we try to wipe it out completely. I believe that there have been many good, valuable elements in our naturecentric traditions, the kinds of heritage which we do not want to see disappear. The Oriental way of appreciating the beauty of nature, of learning from nature, and of being with nature must be preserved, especially in view of the fact that the process of modernization, more often than not, destroys it and brings forth a detrimental ecological imbalance.

How can we then love nature without venerating it? The best possible way to resolve the problem is by the acceptance of the biblical concept of nature, the theocentric view that nature was created by God and was entrusted to man. The acceptance of the Lordship of God upon nature and of our stewardship over it will not make us worship it (the old Oriental way), nor will it make us destroy nature (the modern Western way). We do not own it. Nor do we have any right to destroy it at will. Our proper relation with nature is to manage it well and to make it even more productive and beautiful for the glory of God. By accepting the ownership of God, we as His stewards can restore the image of the Garden of Eden on earth. With this lofty biblical concept of man's relationship with nature, we Asians shall be able to keep on industrializing our countries without necessarily repeating the same destruction of nature as Western people have done.

At this crucial transitional era in which our traditional concept of nature is fast eroding and in which the Western concept of conquering nature appears abhorrent, it is an opportune time for Asian Christians to propagate the biblical concept of God's Lordship of nature and man's stewardship over it. By so doing, we can sublimate some, if not all, of the ethical principles stemming from our ancient traditions which are not incompatible with the Bible. For instance, the principles of filial piety and respecting the old are natural as well as biblical. The Bible says that God gave man reasoning power, a special faculty with which he can mull over things and comprehend their final effects. Our ancestors made the most of their reason by observing nature and drawing some immutable moral principles; but now, by accepting theocentrism, we shall be able to augment the shortcomings of human reasoning power. With God on top of our new moral principles, we Asians can perfect the aspirations of filial piety and veneration of the old which were the core principles of Confucianism. Without negating these principles, we can sublimate them and incorporate them into our new spiritual environment.

Second, to do away with naturecentrism does not mean that we must accept, as most Asian peoples do these days, the technocentrism of the West. With the dazzling speed of technological progress constantly transforming lifestyles to conform to its principles, the Western societies have become exceedingly *technical*. The dominance of technology on the Western man today is different from that of the past not only in degree, but also in kind. Technology is more than something "mechanical." In addition to mechanical engineering, technology today deals with planetary engineering, global engineering, biological engineering, social engineering, political engineering, and even human engineering. Harvey Cox calls today's West "the technopolitan," Zbigniew Brzezinski "the technotronic society," and Marshall McLuhan "the electronic society." Are we Asians then trying to do away with naturecentrism and instead to embrace the technocentrism of the contemporary West?

There is no use repeating that the process of total *technical dominance* has been a mixture of blessings and curses. It has brought more of the latter—according to the writings of Jacques Ellul, Hannah Arendt, and Herbert Marcuse—than the former. In spite of the many advantages that technology has brought forth for us to enjoy, we cannot be blinded to the brutal reality that it has increasingly dehumanized and robotized the Western man and is now attempting to do the same in the East. Because of this more than anything else, we Asians cannot, and should not, accept the cult of technology presently prevalent in the West. The worship of technology is almost as bad as, perhaps even worse than, the cult of nature worship.

However, here again, I do not mean to imply in any way that Christianity is against technological development. On the contrary, the opposite has been the case. The Biblical concept of man's relationship with nature helped man demythologize nature, thereby laying an intellectual foundation for the development of technology. By following God's instructions, Noah, for instance, constructed the ark, demonstrating a knowledge of ship-building technology which amazes even today. Technology, like money, is not inherently good or evil. It can be good or bad according to what purpose it is being used.

Therefore, the proper attitude of Christians toward technology is not to venerate it or to disdain it. To recognize God's sovereignty over all things is an essential prerequisite before we can dethrone technology from its position of omnipotence. Technology must be used for the glory of God in order for it to benefit man.

In this respect, we Asians may have a strong chance of creating a new modern civilization in which technology becomes the servant of man, instead of man serving technology. By so doing, we may not commit the carnal sin of worshiping technology as many Western people have done. The creation of an industrial society dominated by technological know-how and technological principles should not be our goal in modernization. Instead we must aim at creating a new society in which highly developed technology will be subservient to human needs. Technology cannot be an end in itself, but must always be a means to an end, which is the advancement of God's Kingdom.

Third, the instillment of theocentrism in our new spiritual milieu in Asia will guard us from the pitfalls of anthropocentrism and at the same time will enable us to fulfill the aspirations of humanism. To those who do not comprehend the spiritual dimension of our life my assertion may sound illogical and irrational. To men of worldly wisdom, theocentrism may appear to be a return to the Dark Ages. To them the Christian belief in God's sovereignty over all beings on earth may appear to be a way to destroy all the traces of humanity and human dignity in our life. But in fact the opposite has been true.

History is full of cases which demonstrate the paradoxical truth that those who love God, believe in Christ, and have the Holy Spirit in their hearts sacrificially give their lives to the cause of humanity. Those who obey God's commandments cannot stop loving their fellowmen. The best way of serving the Lord is not merely by giving money to church construction, but by taking active service in humanitarian work.

Herein lies the inexorable linkage between evangelization and the expansion of humanity. Without the Holy Spirit residing in a man's mind and directing his life, how can any man love his fellow human beings as his brothers and sisters? I believe that the highest ideal of Buddhism, compassion, is possible when a man accepts Christ as his Savior and tries to serve humanity as the Lord demonstrated through accepting the suffering of the cross. Therefore, evangelization which is the act of making the Gospel—the Good News—known to men and women will be the best possible way to make a man conscious of the suffering of his fellowmen and enable him to partake in the cross of Jesus for the sake of mankind. The recurrent, vexing problems of racism, chauvinism, and all other kinds of conflict in our world can be greatly reduced, if not resolved, by our accepting the Gospel.

Suffice it to say that Christian theocentrism is the only way to fulfill the desires and aspirations of naturecentrism, anthropocentrism, and technocentrism. I assert that it is the only way of avoiding the growth of nihilism, especially in the advanced and advancing societies. By believing in the Lordship of God in time and in space and by acknowledging His Providence in human history, we can see the meaning of life, individually and socially.

However, a caution is necessary at this point. I am not one of those who propose the theory that we must turn our clock back to the medieval West. As a historian, I think that medieval

West was far from being perfectly theocentric. Ignorant of scientific knowledge and living in an indigent stage of agrarian life, the Europeans of the Middle Ages lived in faith as well as in superstition. The residue of naturecentrism coming down from Germanic traditions mixed with Christian teachings. Their veneration of relics and saints, holy or otherwise, attests to their superstitious, unbiblical way of life. But in spite of their superstition, the seeds of real life—the teachings of the Bible—were growing in the Middle Ages. Combined with the efforts of the religious reformers of the sixteenth century (who tried to revive the biblical teachings of the early churches), this spurred social progress and eventually gave birth to modernization in the West.

In brief, our effort to inculcate theocentrism in the new spiritual milieu of Asia is therefore not only a return to the past, especially to the spirit of the Reformation era, but also a leap into the future by synthesizing the cultural elements of the past with those of the present, both of the East and the West, for the glory of God. When, for instance, Oriental music is restructured to express the glory of God, it can be useful for furthering the Kingdom of God. When the highly developed humanistic ethical code of old China is reinterpreted in the light of the Christian theocentrism, it can be very useful in the future society of mankind. By sublimating the superior heritages of all the peoples of Asia, we may succeed in creating a new spiritual milieu on which the future civilization of mankind may be founded. Also, through our efforts to establish the image of the Kingdom of God in our societies, we Asians can stimulate Western Christian brethren to reevaluate their own past in the light of their invaluable spiritual tradition, which they are so carelessly throwing away.

2. TRANSFIGURATION OF THE SOCIAL MILIEU

Spirit expresses itself in the human milieu, materially and socially. Our effort to evangelize the Asian peoples—

whether it will be wholly successful or not—will eventually exert significant changes in our respective societies.

But at this point we have arrived at a serious, controversial question which demands our immediate attention. As seen in the early chapters, the Asian societies are undergoing fundamental, revolutionary changes. A great variety of revolutions—social, political, economic, feminine, generational, psychological, sexual, and intellectual—are going on simultaneously. Are we Asian Christians to sit still with our hands folded behind our backs as though we see nothing, hear nothing, and say nothing? Or are we to jump into social activities and involve ourselves in all sorts of actions? At this point, I have little desire to get myself involved in the endless polemic issues raised by the two contending schools—the other-worldly school that sees Christian efforts confined entirely to going to heaven, and the this-worldly school which equates Christianity with social revolution. Already, on a number of occasions I have expressed my personal view about them. Both are wrong and fall short of being biblical.

Christianity is not, and should not be, other-worldly. After all, the whole universe, according to the Bible, was the handiwork of the Almighty God. The helm of history is in God's hand. Society is no exception, for nothing can exist outside the realm of His grace. Of course, in no way do I deny that the Bible has, throughout the centuries, condemned "the world," the community of sinful men and women in rebellion against God; but God, on the other hand, "so loved the world that He gave his only begotten Son" (John 3:16).

As the children of God, we Christians should often be critical of the ways of modern life, which in general has become so anthropocentric. With keen, observing eyes we should see the ungodly situation of our age and raise criticism reprimanding the sins of the world; but this fact does not automatically make us holy. Until we unite with the Lord, none of us can be wholly free from sin. By the same token, we do not have the license to condemn the society in which we live. Like shepherds, our role is to watch over the well-being of people, believers and unbelievers alike, in the spirit of being "our brothers' keepers."

In this respect, I believe that Christian eschatology is miles apart from the traditional Asian theory of "the end of the world." Whereas in Asia pessimistic people often cursed the world as something inherently doomed to destruction, Christian eschatological thought gives us realistic eyes to see the true condition of the world, and at the same time gives us a new hope of expecting the Second Coming of Christ. Hope, therefore, characterizes our faith. Christian eschatology constantly spurs us to do our utmost for His Kingdom while living on earth. Anyone who tries to remain totally detached from mundane affairs shall be abominable in the eyes of God. On the contrary, those who are diligently serving men and women in need for the sake of the Kingdom of God shall be delivered first when Christ comes again.

On the other hand, Christianity is not, and should not be, this-worldly. During His ministry, at no time did Christ identify His Kingdom with any human society. Any social system existing in historical time is ephemeral. Nothing in the world will remain unchanged. The ultimate goal of human history goes beyond history, beyond mundane affairs, beyond what we can create on earth. The aim of the Christian life cannot, and should not, be social welfare, scientific and technological development, modernization, or the realization of a "postindustrial" society.

Nor can we, I believe, realize an ideal society by taking direct part in the social actions of any revolutionary movement that is based on utopian blueprints. Even if we Christians take political action in our efforts to bring forth a sane society, or even if we take hold of political power in the government and direct national policies at will, we cannot realize an ideal society in historical time. Negatively, we might succeed in toppling a government, but we will find it well-nigh impossible to establish a new one entirely free from vice and corruption.

I believe that Christianity is worldly and unworldly at the same time. As Christians, we must be socially conscious but detach ourselves from political action as an independent group. By seeking to realize the Kingdom of God which lies both within and without the temporal realms of human history, we Christians can spearhead social progress. By being unworldly, we can therefore be most worldly. Any artificial efforts to dichotomize Christianity into two conflicting schools as mentioned earlier can be misleading because the Gospel transcends both; but simultaneously, it combines both.

A man's decision to accept Christ as his Savior is personal, and often appears other-worldly. It seems to possess no social significance whatsoever. But seen over a long time-span, a man's becoming a Christian is bound to have social consequences. With the Holy Spirit residing in him, he will soon translate his faith into action. The change he thus shows in his daily decisions and in his social life cannot help but exert a far-reaching influence upon the society where he lives. During the Middle Ages, even a hermit living in a remote monastery nevertheless spilled his influence over the walls of his secluded community.

Some die-hard followers of the Social Gospel might come out against my position, saying that every individual is societal. No individual can exist independently inasmuch as a person is, after all, a social product. From the very time of birth, an individual gets his habits, language, culture, and other modes of life from his family and from his society. The question of the relative importance of the individual as opposed to society appears, if we are to accept the theories proposed by the Social Gospel, to be infinitesimal. It looks as though changing social institutions should have our first priority, far above the urgency of the evangelization of the individual soul.

But I disagree. Reading the Bible I find, time and again,

that the individual not society is the basic moral unit, the unit which will ultimately stand before God at the last judgment. God judges the iniquity of a society or a civilization in historical time, but nowhere in the Bible do I read that a society will be judged in the last day. Seen in this light, we must first direct our efforts toward evangelizing men and women and only afterward toward reforming social institutions. Trying to change society before preaching the Gospel to individuals is putting the cart before the horse.

On the other hand, it goes without saying that attempting to increase the mere size of the Christian population makes little sense if these believers are so nominal or so unworldly that they refuse to serve their fellowman. A true believer is the one who constantly translates what he believes into action. What we need, most urgently and imperatively, is a growing number of Christians whose lives balance these two extremes in a harmony, without leaning to one end of the pole unduly. Such a balance requires no art of living, but on the contrary demands true faith in action.

On the individual plane, we Asian Christians should take up the role of salt and light in all walks of life. There are 10,000 different kinds of jobs in Japan today and in Korea there are over 6,000. In line with this phenomenal intensification of the division of labor, Asian Christians should take up all sorts of jobs in their respective societies; but needless to say, our profession is the secondary job and our primary job is to work as instruments of God in realizing His Kingdom in this particular age. If, therefore, Christians are trained to take up all these diversified jobs, we need more Christian engineers, Christian doctors, Christian professors, Christian diplomats, Christian statesmen, Christian workers, Christian farmers, Christian social workers, Christian writers, Christian painters, Christian musicians, and so on. However, we should maintain a unity in diversity. In spite of the apparent differences in job description, our primary job—the preaching of the Gospel in our respective positions—is the same. No job, in this respect, is more

important or less important than others. No position is
superior to others. Every Christian, in the eyes of God, is
commissioned to do the same, namely, to proclaim the
Gospel in the calling to which he has been chosen.

To be salt in the place where a Christian works is to
prevent the social organization from being corrupted. In
shining a beacon light upon the community, he will set a
high model for others to emulate. But in any case, we Christians must be His followers seven days a week, instead of
praising Him with our lips in church only once in a week.
The "Seven-day Christian Movement" must be a guiding
goal in our lives, especially in Asia where Christians constitute a social minority group. Though our numbers are
small, our sphere of influence spreads like oil on the water.
No force can really stop us from growing and spreading.

Personally, I don't believe in social organizations composed solely of Christians and directed solely to achieve
Christian aims. As we see the predicament of the Italian
Christian Democratic Party today, if a Christian organization in achieving social objectives fails to live up to its manifested aims, the whole Christian community might be
blamed in consequence. Instead, I urge every Asian Christian to take part actively in the various social groups presently emergent in the wake of industrialization. As the agrarian stage of social development evolves into a more advanced and more complex industrial society, the whole social structure changes. The old primary groups—such as
clans or the idyllic village community—give way to the new
secondary groups—such as labor unions, trade unions, professional associations, or political parties. Therefore, it is
high time, the most opportune time, for Asian Christians to
take an active part in these newly rising organizations and
instill a Christian spirit in them.

Furthermore, I see the necessity of having some loose
organizations of Christians in the same profession, such as
Christian businessmen's associations or Christian teachers'
fellowships, not so much to achieve any narrowly defined

aims as to share friendship among themselves. Possibly such organizations can be organized either locally, nationally, or internationally. Especially I favor the idea of forming such fellowship associations on a regional level so as to stimulate each other on a regional scale. Also, having national chapters of such organizations as the Gideons can be very rewarding. We thus may learn much from the experiences of our Western Christian brethren.

In my view, likewise, the role of the Christian church in social problems must be dual—active and negative at the same time. The church is in human society but stands above it. The church, as the image of God's Kingdom on earth, must stand aloof from mundane affairs, but this fact should not be used as a justification for being escapist. I believe that the church should play the role of the Old Testament prophets, i.e., it should be a voice in the wilderness. Representing the voice of God, it should be the conscience of human society. Constantly, without ceasing, the church should reprimand the wrongdoings of social institutions.

I firmly believe that this is precisely the cause for which Asian churches should fight. The main task of the church is to save individual souls through the grace of God, but its mission does not end there. By pursuing this God-given mission, the church can radiate a healthy, wholesome influence upon society. The Gospel has power not only to save individuals from eternal death, but also to save societies from degeneration. To deviate from this course by turning to the Social Gospel movement or to spiritual escapism will lead us down the wrong road. Asian Christians must be united by this common cause and work cooperatively to accomplish this God-given mission.

In the hierarchy of values with God on the very top, everything else becomes subordinate to God's sovereign power. When politicians, with a deep awareness of their God-given mission, work to realize the Kingdom of God in the realm of politics, the ideals of democracy can be, partially if not wholly, achieved. In politics, what is needed most is not liberty or equality among peoples, but the righteousness of God. If the righteousness of God prevails in a society, political freedom will be maximized as a consequence. By the same token, if businessmen live up to the ideal of Christian stewardship in handling their property, the ideals expressed by both capitalism and socialism can be realized. By rendering to God what He rightly owns, we gain all the material blessings.

Science should be subservient to the will of God, working for man's benefit, rather than for its own self-propagation. Art must not be for art's sake, but for the glory of God. Like Handel's *Messiah*, when a composer communes with the undying beauty of God's Kingdom, he can compose supremely pleasing music. If a painter sees, with his spiritual eyes, a glimpse of His Kingdom, he becomes capable of painting masterpieces, like those of Leonardo da Vinci's *Last Supper*, which will be acclaimed for their aesthetic beauty for ages to come. By constantly striving to achieve things for God's glory, we can be productive in all realms of human life, be they economic, social, political, scientific, or artistic.

Our faith in God makes us become theocentric in our spiritual life, which in turn enables us to synthesize conflicting social forces and divergent cultural elements onto a new plane, a new dimension of life. Unlike the Marxist concept of historical materialism which leaves the process of dialectical change in history to the impersonal laws of chance—although the Communists ignore this and do their best to brood revolution in all societies of the world—Christians believe that a real transfiguration of history, if we can use the term in a secularized sense, comes from the direct intervention of God in human history. At the same time, we believe that God uses human beings, especially his faithful children, in changing and directing the history of mankind. This is to say that by surrendering our entire lives to the cause of the kingdom of God and allowing ourselves to be used as His instruments, we can write new chapters in human history geared to a genuine "progress."

Over the years as a student of history, I have come to a firm conviction that human history makes true progress when we Christians truly become ahistorical. As more and more people seek to become part of the Kingdom of God which lies above and beyond our mundane world, the true and proper development of society comes as a byproduct. On the other hand, when people attempt to make historical progress solely on the basis of some humanly conceived utopian blueprints, the progress they seek turns against them, eventually bringing forth all sorts of human miseries. Look at what happened in Germany under Hitler's megalomaniac dream. Look at the growing chaos in today's Red China.

The reasons for this phenomenon are too obvious to be discussed in detail. If human beings were omnipotent and all-wise, their schemes and designs for the future could be perfect. But being in reality so short-sighted, blinded, limited, and sinful, we have no way to see into the future. Without the grace of God, human history cannot be sustained. The world without His continuing providence, must already be a great inferno. But at the same time people, being created in the image of God, can be genuinely creative by surrendering themselves to be His instruments working in history for the realization of His Kingdom.

In brief, what we Asians need more than anything else at this historical stage is the transfiguration—a positive creation of a new age through synthesizing the heritages of East and West—of our spiritual, social, cultural milieu. But this cannot be done by identifying ourselves with any of the sociopolitical ideologies. Instead, this can be done through our working for the realization of the Kingdom of God in our lives—on an individual, social, and global scale.

Hegel was right when he said that human history is a revelation of spirit. But it is not a revelation of the spirit of men and women or of the *Weltgeist*. It is the combined spirit of God and men; or in other words, God's Spirit—the Holy Spirit—residing in our spirit.

Some thinkers have tried to separate history into two opposing realms, divine and profane. Many philosophers speculated about these two categories of history as though they existed in two entirely different realms. But this is not so. God is the Lord of all history, secular or otherwise. He uses the rise and fall of great empires—Babylon, Assyria, Greece, Rome, Great Britain, the United States, the Soviet Union, Red China, and others—for furthering His purposes. Secular history cannot, therefore, be left out of His domain, but it is abundantly clear that it is a subsidiary and not the main stream of world history. In the same vein, it is equally clear that the kind of progress that secular history elicits cannot be eternal in value, only ephemeral. We can only make progress when we completely surrender our will to the will of the Lord of history.

3. CALLING AND RESPONSE

The most important question ahead of us is, therefore, not how well we can theoretically prove the preeminence of the Kingdom of God which lies far above and beyond secular ideologies, but how to apply this cardinal principle in our daily life. How should each one of us respond to His calling? How should my local church respond to His calling? How can our Christian churches throughout Asia be awakened to this new mission? We have no reason to be apologetic about this biblical truth. We are born to Asia to do our utmost for the realization of His Kingdom in our respective societies.

On a spatial plane, the Kingdom of God begins in one individual life. Each Asian Christian is commissioned to live and die for His Kingdom. With whatever God-given talents one has, it is one's responsibility to develop, cultivate, and fulfill them for the cause of Christ. For instance, I have no way to know fully why I was born in Korea in this age, but I believe that it must have been part of God's plan for me to work in Korea for the realization of His Kingdom. I was "thrown into" the twentieth century for no other reason than to serve His Kingdom in these hopeless times. How wonderful it is to be called of God for His service! 1 Corinthians 1:26 says, "For ye see your calling, brethren, how that not many wise men after the flesh, not many mighty, not many noble, are called." Ephesians 1:18 says, "The eyes of your understanding being enlightened; that ye may know what is the hope of his calling, and what the riches of the glory of his inheritance in the saints." I am not wise, nor mighty or noble but He has called me to His work and "enlightened" my eyes to understand the hope of His calling. 2 Timothy 1:9 again states that God "called us with an holy calling, not according to our works, but according to his own purpose and grace."

However, very often I find myself resisting His calling. Like Moses, I feel that I am not qualified to meet His expectations. Like Moses, I think that people "will not believe me, nor hearken unto my voice" (Exodus 4:1). Like Moses, I should like to tell God, "Lord, please! Send someone else" (Exodus 4:13). The reason for my denial of His calling is due more to my feelings of inadequacy than my seeking worldly things. Simply I do not have courage to bear the burden expected of me. Ephesians 4:1 says, "Ye walk worthy of the vocation wherewith ye are called," but I find myself totally unworthy.

In our days, many scholars say that in order to be a leader a man must possess great physical energy, superb courage, deep insights, tact and humor, skill of organization, personal magnetism, and unending persistence; but I possess none of these qualities. How can I be a leader in the works of God? I find, however, that God did not call me to be a leader, but He called me to be His servant. What I need is not leadership training, but servanthood training. What I have to worry about is not to lead men and women, but to serve them in the name of Christ. In Christian works, we have only one leader, namely Jesus Christ, and none other. I neither can nor should become a leader. But when a man serves Him faithfully, God lifts him up to become a true leader among men and women. This is a paradoxical truth, the secret of Christian leadership.

Paul, for instance, called himself a servant of the Lord. Never did he seek to be a leader. He gave up his carnal desires for God's glory. Ambitious for Christ, and not for himself, Paul gave everything he possessed to the cause of God's Kingdom, even to taking up the cross; as a result, he gained everything. His fame as a Christian leader rose as time went by. Even in the purely worldly sense, Paul was not a loser because he, through his unsurpassing theocentric life, earned what millions of people could not even dream of. We respect and admire Paul as a Christian leader because he lived his life as a most faithful servant of Christ.

The Bible tells us that Peter, another example, was a very cowardly man, a man who in spite of following Jesus for three years denied knowing the Lord three times. He became brave and courageous not through his own strength but through the power of the Holy Spirit. Only after receiving the Holy Spirit did he become a great servant of our Master.

The Holy Spirit, filling our minds, makes us courageous and bold, and enables us to maximize our potential. Then we can fully express our talents for the cause of His Kingdom. The Holy Spirit residing in us guides us into all truth (John 16:13). He directs us in the selection of options. He comforts us when we become discouraged. Without relying on the Holy Spirit, we can do nothing.

Also, when we have the Holy Spirit in our minds, we become aware of the cardinal truth that our bodies are not our own. 1 Corinthians 3:16 says, "Know ye not that ye are the temple of God, and that the Spirit of God dwelleth in you?" Physical fitness is not for our happiness alone. By being fit physically, we can work harder for the Lord. Christian servants must maintain their health, for they do not own their bodies. Everything, including one's body, belongs to the Lord; by surrendering his body, a man can truly enjoy his physical happiness as well.

If each one of us is to be faithful to His calling, we must persistently and perpetually renew, regenerate, and transfigure our individual life so as to be filled with the Holy Spirit. Without human capability and knowledge, we cannot achieve anything positively worthwhile, but through obeying the Holy Spirit, everything—however impossible the task appears to be—can be accomplished. By constantly praying, searching for the truth in the Bible, witnessing about Christ in season and out of season, and by fellowshipping with Christian brethren, each one of us may continue to grow in the Holy Spirit. Regardless of our individual professions, our primary job is the same, namely, the realization of the Kingdom of God. The life of Christ as described in the Bible is the model for us to imitate.

Then, and only then, can we have an immutable moral compass in our individual lives, a compass which will direct our daily decisions so as not to make us fall into sin. Our daily decisions will be made on the basis of the moral compass shown to us by the Holy Spirit. "Am I trying to please God or to please me?" "Will this decision serve God's purpose or mine?" "Am I really trying to realize the Kingdom of God or my own carnal desires?" These are some of the questions that we will individually ask ourselves before finalizing any decision.

Individual efforts must then be channeled into a collective effort toward achieving social, economic, political, and cultural goals that make His sovereign power a reality. When our efforts create a balance between individuality and collectivity in the Christian life, the theological controversy between individual salvation and the Social Gospel will be resolved. As the great men of faith such as Luther and Calvin endeavored to transfigure their individual lives and their societies, so we must strive for the realization of the Kingdom of God in our hearts and in society alike.

Likewise, our church must be regenerated and transfigured in a state of perpetual revolution. In the light of the Bible, our church must constantly try to follow its God-given mission. In this respect, our Asian churches should ward off the danger of becoming Shamanized. The church should not be a place like the old Buddhist temples or the Shinto shrines where people try to solicit the divine to give them material blessings. We do not go to seek physical blessings or spiritual consolation. The assurance of salvation that we have received through accepting Christ in our minds is already the greatest blessing one can hope for. The reason we assemble in the church as a group is to praise God, stimulate each other in Christian fellowship, and work for His Kingdom.

The sovereignty of God must be reasssserted constantly in our church. No pastor, no elder, no rich businessman, no powerful politician, and no great intellectual giant should dominate church activities. The church must not be used as an instrument for furthering human ambition. The Lordship of God over the church is essential if the church is to fulfill its mission on earth. By being truly theocentric, the church can really serve humanity.

Ultimately, we may bring forth the unity of Asia. The unity we see should not stem from "human coercion but from the drawing power of the Spirit." It must be "active unity—a functional unity."[4] That being the case, the evangelization of Asian peoples is a prerequisite for the unity of Asia we hope to realize. Without evangelization, no institutional unity among Asian peoples can be possible. In this sense, it is high time for us Asian Christians to be missionary conscious. The task of preaching the Gospel must not be limited to our home countries but spill over our national boundaries; our efforts for evangelization must reach out to the rest of Asia. The age of Western-dominated, Western-based, Western-directed missionary work is over. We Asian Christians must be aware of our own responsibility and should find ways and means to coordinate our ef-

forts in missionary activities. Already, the churches of
Korea and Japan have sent out missionaries to Southeast
Asia.

However, the mere change of faces—from those of Western missionaries to those of Asian missionaries—cannot be
sufficient to meet the needs. Mission strategies and tactics
must be changed in accordance with the rapidly changing
situation of each locality. At the same time, we Asian Christians must guard ourselves from falling into the pitfall of the
cardinal sin—the sin of pride. This is no time for us to bear
an attitude of "we-know-better-than-you" towards Western missionaries who are still actively working in Asia. Nor
do we wish to underrate the meritorious achievements of
Western churches in bringing us the Gospel. In the same
vein, I do not subscribe to the idea of partnership between
the Asian churches and the Western churches—the kind of
partnership which tries to combine Western money and
Asian manpower.

I personally believe that the time has come for us to work
out a new form of partnership in evangelizing Asia, hopefully on the basis of global familism. On equal footing, in
the spirit of the brotherhood in God, the Western churches
and the Asian churches would join hand in hand to pool our
material and human resources. Matthew 12:25 says, "Every
kingdom divided against itself is brought to desolation; and
every city or house divided against itself shall not stand."
For the sake of the Kingdom of God, we Christians of both
the East and the West must be united, thereby opening a
new era of concerted missionary activities.

However, harmony and unity cannot be attained without
conscious effort and hard work. An American professor observed the spirit of unity among Japanese people—the
yamato spirit—in a puppet show. If five or six puppets are
to perform a show on a stage, about an equal number of
manipulators behind the curtain have to be completely
like-minded. If five or six persons are to attain complete
unity of mind, they have to endure rigid training for at least

three years by living and practicing together. In order to open a new era of missionary work, an era in which we may even venture into Red China to preach the Gospel, in which we might open doors in Indo-China and also in North Korea, we Asian Christians must be trained to work with Western Christian brethren jointly and cooperatively, on equal footing, in brotherly love. Let us train ourselves to be worthy of His calling.

In so doing, we may even realize the age-old dream of man—the realization of one world civilization with the peoples of different cultures united under one omnipotent and omnipresent God. Making manifest the hierarchy of values based upon the recognition of God's sovereignty over all men will be the surest way to avoid the impending holocaust and to pave ways toward a historical transfiguration for all mankind.

Conclusion

The situation in Asia today is chaotic, so confusing that no one, however perspicacious, can find direction in the future. The age of ideologies which long characterized the postwar era is about to be over, but no new "secular gospel" is in sight. Liberal democracy, Communism, socialism, nationalism, and many other kinds of sociopolitical ideologies have produced all sorts of undesirable by-products and are fast becoming defunct.

According to the Bible, only the Kingdom of God can give us answers to present problems. It teaches us how to become a member of this eternal Kingdom, how to work with our fellowmen for the common cause of His Kingdom, and how to realize it, piece by piece and bit by bit, in our social and spiritual milieu. By seeking to realize the divine milieu in our society, individually and collectively, we can goad historical progress. In so doing we will bring forth true unity in Asia and the world.

God is calling you and me. He wants to make us His change-agents. Shall we respond to His calling with a big yes? We must reaffirm our dedication to the Kingdom of God and to the transfiguring power of the Spirit by constantly remembering this key biblical passage: "Seek ye first the kingdom of God, and his righteousness, and all these things shall be added unto you" (Matthew 6:33).

Notes

CHAPTER ONE

1. Dick Wilson, *Asia Awakes* (Middlesex, England: Penguin Books, 1973), p. 118.

2. Ibid., p. 31.

3. Carl J. Friedrich, ed., *Revolution* (New York: Atherton Press, 1967), p. 132.

4. Robert Sinai, *The Challenge of Modernization* (New York: W.W. Norton, 1964), p. 47.

5. Friedrich, *Revolution*, p. 186.

6. Sinai, *Challenge*, pp. 64-5.

7. *Kyonghyang Shinmun* [The Kyonghyang Daily Press in Korean], April 28, 1965.

8. Koryo University, *Minzok Munhwa Yonku* [A study of national culture—in Korean], vol. 1, October, 1967. p. 1.

9. A. F. K. Organski, *The Stages of Political Development* (New York: Alfred Knopf, 1965), pp. 20-185.

10. Wilson, *Asia Awakes*, p. 17.

11. Ibid., p. 24.

12. Yamamoto Kyoshi, *Bummei no Kuzo to Hendo* [The structure and change of civilization] (Tokyo: Sobunshia, 1961), pp. 100-5.

13. Kenneth Boulding, "Post-Civilization," in Melvin Cherno, ed., *The Contemporary World Since 1850* (New York: McGraw-Hill, 1967), p. 573.

14. As quoted in Gordon Wright, ed., *An Age of Controversy* (New York: Dodd, Mead and Co., 1968), p. 479.

15. Wilson, *Asia Awakes*, pp. 176-80.

16. Ibid.

CHAPTER TWO

1. Arnold Toynbee, *A Study of History* (London: Oxford University Press, 1969), vol. 9, pp. 220-306.

2. William Theodore DeBary, *The Buddhist Tradition* (New York: Vintage Books, 1972), p. xcii-iii.

3. William Theodore DeBarry, ed., *Sources of Chinese Tradition* (New York: Columbia University Press, 1968), p. 458.

4. Jung Young Lee, *Patterns of Inner Process* (Secaucus, N.J.: The Citadel Press, 1976), p. 30.

5. Ibid., p. 49.

6. As quoted by Grace E. Cairns, *Philosophies of History* (New York: Philosophical Library, 1962), p. 167.

7. DeBarry, *Chinese Tradition*, p. 33.

8. Gustav A. Wetter, *Dialectical Materialism*, trans. P. Heath (London: Routledge and Kegan Paul, 1958), p. 4.

9. Ibid., p. 283.

10. Ibid.

11. Ibid.

12. Ibid., pp. 322-3.

13. Ibid., p. 356.

14. Karl Marx and Friedrich Engels, *Manifesto of the Communist Party*, Great Books of the Western World (Chicago: Encyclopedia Britannica, 1952), vol. 50, pp. 415-34.

15. Harold Martin and Richard Ohmann, ed., *Inquiry and Expression* (New York: Holt, Rinehart and Winston, 1958), p. 35.

16. Ibid., pp. 35-6.

17. Ibid., pp. 39-42.

18. Patrick Gardiner, *Theories of History* (New York: The Free Press, 1959), p. 175.

19. Paul Edwards, *A Modern Introduction to Philosophy* (New York: The Free Press, 1965), p.

20. Gardiner, *Theories of History*, p. 143.

21. Edwards, *Modern Introduction to Philosophy*, p. 5.

22. Ibid.

23. Ibid., p. 7.

24. Toynbee, *Study of History*, 9:348.

25. Hans Meyerhoff, ed., *The Philosophy of History in Our Time* (New York: Doubleday, 1959), pp.301-4.

26. Ibid., pp. 293-7.

27. H.J. Blackham, *Six Existentialist Thinkers* (London: Routledge and Kegan Paul, 1961), p. 88.

28. Edwards, *Modern Introduction to Philosophy*, p. 174.

29. *The Nutall Dictionary of Quotations* (London: Frederick Warne and Co., 1970), p. 262.

30. Ernst Cassirer, *An Essay on Man* (New Haven: Yale University Press, 1944), pp. 24-5.

31. *A Handbook of Christian Theology* (Cleveland: The World Publishing Co., 1963), p. 357.

32. Albert Dondeyne, *Faith and the World* (Pittsburgh: Duquesne University Press, 1963), p. 78.

33. Ibid., pp. 75-6.

34. Ibid., p. 78.

35. George Schweitzer, *Greek and Hebrew Elements in the Origin of Modern Science*, an unpublished monograph, 1969.

36. Ninian Smart, *The Religious Experience of Mankind* (New York: Charles Scribner's Sons, 1968), p. 3.

37. John B. Magee, *Religion and Modern Man* (New York: Harper and Row, 1967), pp. 244-5.

38. Schweitzer, *Origin of Modern Science*, p. 2.

39. Paul Tillich, *Theology and Culture* (London: Oxford University Press, 1968), pp. 35-6.

40. J. H. Hexter, *Tradition of Western Thought* (Chicago: Rand McNally, 1967), p. 7.

41. Franklin Baumer, "Twentieth-century Version of the Apocalypse," in W. Warren Wagar, ed., *European Intellectual History Since Darwin and Marx* (New York: Harper Torchbooks, 1967), pp. 133-4.

42. Toynbee, *Study of History*, 9:403.

43. Reinhold Niebuhr, *The Nature and Destiny of Man* (New York: Charles Scribner's Sons, 1953), pp. 1-100.

44. Wright, *Age of Controversy* pp. 488-9.

45. C. Virgil Gheorghiu, *The Twenty-Fifth Hour*, trans. R. Eldon (London: The Windmill Press, 1950), p. 43.

46. William Huhns, *The Post-Industrial Prophets* (New York: Weybright and Talley), 1971, p. 1.

47. Harold Dewolf, *Responsible Freedom* (New York: Harper and Row, 1951), pp. 50-149.

48. Myron Weiner, *Modernization: The Dynamics of Growth* (New York: Basic Books, 1969), p. 508.

49. Ibid.

50. Max Weber, *Protestant Ethics and the Spirit of Capitalism*, trans. into Korean by Kwon Sei-won (Seoul: Ilchogak, 1963), pp. 49-90.

51. Arnold Toynbee, *A Study of History*, abridged by D. C. Somervell (New York: Oxford University Press, 1961), pp. 225-6.

52. Werner Sombart, *The Jews and Modern Capitalism* (New York: Macmillan Co., 1962), *passim*.

53. Richard Niebuhr, *Christ and Culture* (New Haven: Yale University Press, 1957), pp. 54-95.

54. Ibid.

55. Jacob Burckhardt, *The Civilization of the Renaissance in Italy* (New York: Harper and Row, 1958), vol. 1, p. 34.

56. William Woodruff, *The Impact of Western Man* (New York: St. Martin's Press, 1967), p. 266.

57. Arnold Toynbee, *Civilization on Trial* (Cleveland: The World Publishing Co., 1958), p. 206.

58. Wright, *Age of Controversy*, pp. 488-9.

59. William R. Miller, *The New Christianity* (New York: Dell Publishing Co., 1967), pp. 251-300.

60. Ibid.

61. Ibid.

62. Ibid., pp. 349-51.

63. Ibid., p. 280.

64. Cassirer, *Essay on Man*, pp. 9-14.

65. Wright, *Age of Controversy*, p. 479.

66. Wagar, *European Intellectual History*, p. 191.

67. Wright, *Age of Controversy*, pp. 488-9.

CHAPTER THREE

1. Purnell H. Benson, *Religion in Contemporary Society* (New York: Harper, 1960), p. 697.

2. Ibid., p. 700.

3. Frederick Catherwood, "Reform or Revolution?" in Brian Griffith, ed., *Is Revolution Change:* (London: Inter-Varsity Press, 1972), p. 33.

4. Ibid., p. 97.

5. Ibid.

6. Donald Puchala, *Patterns in Western European Integration*, an unpublished paper presented at the 1970 Annual Meeting of the American Political Science Association, Los Angeles, California.

CHAPTER FOUR

1. *Korea Herald*, June 11, 1977.

2. *Chongsin Daebo*, June 24, 1976.

3. John Haggai, *New Hope for Planet Earth* (Nashville, Tennessee: Thomas Nelson, 1974), p. 103.

4. Ibid., p.17-8.